WHERE YOUR TREASURE IS

THE LAST SPIRITUAL COUNSELS OF A
MODERN MASTER, FATHER ADRIAN VAN KAAM

WHERE YOUR TREASURE IS

THE LAST SPIRITUAL COUNSELS OF A MODERN MASTER, FATHER ADRIAN VAN KAAM

BY SUSAN MUTO
with a foreword by Cardinal Donald Wuerl

LAMBING PRESS | PITTSBURGH

Lambing Press

Copyright © 2018 Susan Muto

All rights reserved.

Published in the United States by Lambing Press.

www.LambingPress.com

ISBN 978-0-9978215-4-3

Book design by Christina Aquilina

It is my honor and joy to dedicate this book to the many students and colleagues who have attended my classes on the ancient, medieval, and modern masters of the spiritual life. Their love for the Christian classics has inspired my teaching and validated the depth of insight found in the life's work and legacy of our mentor in the spiritual life, Father Adrian vVan Kaam, CSSp, PhD (1920-2007). He gifted us with many words of wisdom, and none more memorable than these: *"Remember, the soul you save may be your own, and God knows it's well worth saving."* The prayer he wrote for the Epiphany Association in 2000 gives us a glimpse into his own soul:

Thank you, Lord, for this new day in which you call me to be an epiphany of your care and concern.

Radiate your presence through me in my family, in my places of labor and leisure.

Give me the grace to meet you in the sacrament of everydayness.

Let me share in the beauty of your hidden life in Nazareth.

When I fail, let me experience in joy your forgiveness in which I am immersed always, everywhere. Teach me to turn obstacles and failures, benefits and successes, into formation opportunities.

Strengthen my commitment to be a manifestation of your love and tender mercy. Amen.

TABLE OF CONTENTS

✛⇥⋙⇤✛

FOREWORD
by Cardinal Donald Wuerl

B y definition, Christians are disciples of the Lord Jesus. "In Antioch," Saint Luke tells us, "the disciples were for the first time called Christians" (Acts 11:26). The name "Christian" was a summary description applied to people who were already following a distinctive way of life.

A disciple, as the word suggests, is someone who takes on the *discipline* of a certain school or teacher. You and I, like the original twelve Apostles, are disciples of Jesus. We take up the "yoke" and "burden" that he has offered us (Matthew 11:29-30), and we take it up "daily," as he said we should (Luke 9:23).

It is common today to refer to an individual path of discipleship as one's "spirituality." Christian life has a recognizable core, but our faith finds expression in many different ways. Today, I believe, there is a resurgence of interest in spirituality. The last century presented us with pioneering works by authors of marked ability. I include Adolphe Tanquerey, Réginald Garrigou-Lagrange, and Juan González Arintero—and then, later on, my own teacher Jordan Aumann.

These are authors who charted a way of discipleship for our times. But in order to do that they first had to *be* disciples. They apprenticed themselves to the great teachers of the past, and then they presented the teachings of their spiritual ancestors in a new, accessible, and systematic form. They considered themselves servants of a great tradition, bringing the ancient faith vividly alive for another generation.

When we look for teachers of spirituality today, Dr. Susan Muto certainly has to be included. Her name belongs along with the name of her own teacher, Father Adrian van Kaam, on any list today that speaks about the pedagogy of spirituality.

Dr. Muto has achieved a significant place as a voice of modern spirituality. With Father van Kaam, whom you will come to know in the pages of this book, she founded the Epiphany Association in order to fulfill a desire expressed by Pope Blessed Paul VI. There, Dr. Muto and Father van Kaam worked to integrate the insights and methods of modern psychology with the great heritage of Catholic spirituality. Their work has been providential and inspirational. When historians come to tell the story of the development of spirituality in our time, they will certainly speak of Dr. Susan Muto and Father Adrian van Kaam.

Dr. Muto has written many books, but this may be the purest, clearest, and most essential presentation of her message. Here she speaks with the voice of rich experience. Her message in this book is the heart of Father van Kaam — which aspired to nothing other than the heart of Jesus.

It is to Jesus that we, too, commit ourselves as disciples. We are never alone in the spiritual life, because he is always with us. Yet Jesus told us that he would also send us teachers and shepherds and guides, so that we would never feel orphaned or abandoned. He told us, moreover, that he would build us a Church, where we could encounter saints and scholars, all recognizable as disciples, who would show us the way of discipleship.

In this book, Dr. Muto helps us to see that "spirituality" is never a solitary pursuit. We do not create a spiritual life *ex nihilo* out of our private dreams and wishes. Dr. Muto situates us squarely in the Church of Jesus Christ—in its tradition, with its saints, living its collective life to the fullest.

Jesus often spoke of his doctrine and his kingdom as "treasure" (see, for example, Matthew 6:20-21). As a good disciple of Jesus, Dr. Muto uses the same metaphor to shape this book. And the book itself truly is a treasure.

Cardinal Wuerl is Archbishop of Washington, D.C.

PROLOGUE

＋＊＊＊＋＊

A life that is all head and no heart is as unbalanced as one that is all heart and no head. A truly intellectual life balances the gathering of information with growth in spiritual formation. Our insights and findings need to be as thoughtfully astute as they are spiritually attuned to divine inspiration.

Several months before he left this world, and while he had the stamina to do so, Father Adrian van Kaam afforded me the honor of transcribing a series of short sayings he called his "golden nuggets." Despite his deteriorating physical state, he produced a choice collection of fifty-two of them—one for each week of the year. These treasures emerged from the depths of what he deemed his "crucifying epiphany."

When Father Adrian described his debilitated condition, toward the end of his life, as a "crucifying" or "crucifixion" epiphany, he knew he had found a term to capture the privilege only suffering allows, that of placing ourselves on the cross of love with Jesus Christ himself. Mostly we think of the resurrection—and rightly so—as an epiphany. Easter is the feast of light. It was important to Father Adrian not to associate the cross, by contrast, with darkness, but to see in it the bright light of redemption.

The poetry in his memoirs, written both during and after the war and toward the end of his sojourn on earth, expresses what a grace it was for Father Adrian to suffer with joy. I believe he would not have traded his "crucifying

12

epiphany" for any price. When wellness was no longer possible, he seemed to have reached that place of peace where
all that mattered was to be at one with the crucified Christ.
The light that then shone through this faithful servant of his
was a true epiphany for all who visited him. The cross of
pain had become the source of his greatest gain: to decrease
that Christ might increase.

Each nugget that emerged from the crucible of his end-
of-life condition was, as I assured him, living proof of his
soul-saving choice to abandon himself in peace and joy to
the mystery of love embracing him in time and in faith for
all eternity.

In honor of his life-long immersion in the formative
reading of Scripture and the masters, I will begin each chapter of this book with a selection from one his "nuggets,"
printed in italics. It will then be complemented by a relat-
ed passage from Holy Scripture, followed by reflections of
mine rooted in the literature of spirituality. I offer them to
readers who long to experience renewed intimacy with the
Trinity, not only when they meditate on each chapter but
also when they incorporate what they have learned into
their daily life. Blessed by God's grace, let us pass on these
last spiritual counsels of a modern master. Let us pass on
the teachings of Father Adrian van Kaam to anyone who
seeks the wisdom for living that God bestows upon us in
ways beyond counting.

PART ONE
BEFRIENDED BY THE LORD

✦•❦❧❦•✦

✦•❦❧❦•✦

1. BEING CALLED FRIENDS
The gift of friendship mirrors God's befriending of us.

No one has greater love than this, to lay down one's life for one's friends. You are my friends if you do what I command you. I do not call you servants any longer, because the servant does not know what the master is doing; but I have called you friends, because I have made known to you everything that I have heard from my Father (John 15:13-15).

Between a King and his subjects there is a distance no one would dare to traverse without a formal invitation. Such is not the case with Jesus Christ. So great is the Lord's love for us that he removes the label of servant and replaces it with the word "friend," thereby acknowledging the bond of intimacy only such an encounter can connote. Friends who walk hand in hand through the peaks and valleys of life would not give a second thought to shedding their life's blood for one another, were that sacrifice asked of them. Jesus takes this promise of friendship one step further: he will not only share with us all that the Father has told him; he will also lay down his life for our salvation.

St. Teresa of Avila (1515-1542) enjoyed this bond of befriending with her Divine Master. Of their relationship she wrote in *The Way of Perfection:* "If you grow accustomed to having Him present at your side, and He sees that you do so with love and that you go about striving to please Him, you will not be able—as they say—to get away from Him; He will never fail you; He will help you in all your trials; you will find Him everywhere. Do you think it's some small matter to have a friend like this at your side?"[1]

In one short paragraph, this saint and Doctor of the Church outlines the steps to our accepting the Lord's invitation to be with him in friendship. First of all, we must picture him always at our side. We look upon him with love, work to please him, and become more receptive to his every directive. We trust that he is with us in every trial we have to endure and in every triumph of peace and joy he grants. With such a friend at our side, no demand made of us on the way of Christian perfection ought to deter us.

Such letting be in love teaches us to respond to the movements of grace in the core of our being as well as in the world around us. The blessed awareness of our friendship with one another and with the Lord brings us that much closer to the dream of unity detailed by the Apostle Paul, who says, "For just as the body is one and has many members, and all the members of the body, though many, are one body, so it is with Christ. For in one Spirit we were all baptized into one body—Jews or Greeks, slaves or free— and we were all made to drink of one Spirit" (1 Corinthians 12:12-13).

LET US PRAY

Lord, remind me that my purpose on earth is to enter into a friendship so deep that it enables me to see signs of your love in everyone I meet. Let this revealed knowledge illumine my heart, evoke my compassion for suffering humanity, and grant me a clearer vision of the ways God is with me, his child and dearest companion. May the truth of God's befriending radiate through my whole being and bring me to the awesome awareness that we are one in the spirit and one in the Lord. Amen.

✦❡➣❡✦

2. Healed by Christ's Wounds

The delectable pain of the wound of love is a comfort to my soul.

When he was abused, he did not return abuse; when he suffered, he did not threaten; but he entrusted himself to the one who judges justly. He himself bore our sins in his body on the cross, so that, free from sins, we might live for righteousness; by his wounds you have been healed (1 Peter 2:23-24).

The paradoxes found in this revelation are stunning. A wound by all accounts hurts us and others; it does not heal. Our willful refusal to listen blocks our willingness to be with and for those entrusted to our care. We may be too obtuse to hear their plea for help.

By contrast, Christ returns abuse with forgiveness, unjust cruelty with mercy. He wants neglect to be replaced by neighborliness, but without his help it would be impossible to do so. The rivers of our woundedness run so deep that nothing but the suffering Jesus endured could redeem our sinful condition.

Our crucified Lord did not believe in vengeance or re-

venge. In the face of his accusers, he preferred silent acceptance to vociferous threats. Nailed to a cross that signified
bondage and subjection, he gained our freedom from sin.
As the hour of his death drew near, he begged the Father
to forgive his captors, revealing to the end that sanctity is
never attained without sacrifice.

The Father explains to St. Catherine of Siena (1347-1380)
in her masterpiece, *The Dialogue*, why he allowed Jesus to
live in our company before ascending to heaven to sit at his
right hand. His plan from the beginning was to make of his
Son a bridge between humanity and divinity: "the bridge-
way of his teaching, ... as I told you, is held together by my
power and my Son's wisdom and the mercy of the Holy
Spirit. My power gives the virtue of courage to those who
follow this way. Wisdom gives them light to know the truth
along the way. And the Holy Spirit gives them a love that
uproots all sensual love from the soul and leaves only vir-
tuous love ... through his teaching as much as when he was
among you, he is ... the bridge leading to the very height of
heaven."[2]

The faith Jesus asks of us can never be reduced to a superficial set of moral principles. To trust him to heal our
wounds, we must believe without question in his Word. It
is the medicine that gives meaning to our suffering. Thanks
to his mercy and forgiveness, "we obtained access to this
grace in which we stand; and we boast in our hope of sharing the glory of God. And not only that, but we also boast in
our sufferings, knowing that suffering produces endurance,
and endurance produces character, and character produces
hope and hope does not disappoint us, because God's love
has been poured into our hearts through the Holy Spirit that
has been given to us" (Romans 5:2-5).

LET US PRAY

Lord, this reminder to "hope against hope" is the balm that heals the sting of daily suffering and gives it deeper meaning. The more like Christ I become, the more I experience the call to conversion that grows louder with each passing day. The blessing of affliction is the starting point of my flight to you. Illness, disappointment, the loss of a loved one, the failure of a business—all become invitations to accept what I cannot change and to pray for the courage to change what I can. Give me the grace to allow this "crucifying epiphany" to be the ever-present healing force in my life. Amen.

3. ADVANCING IN WISDOM

To follow the way of wisdom is to live in cordial intimacy with the Trinity.

For wisdom is more mobile than any motion; because of her pureness she pervades and penetrates all things. For she is a breath of the power of God, and a pure emanation of the glory of the Almighty; therefore nothing defiled gains entrance into her. For she is a reflection of eternal light, a spotless mirror of the working of God, and an image of his goodness (Wisdom 7:24-26).

In an age of information, pundits of every persuasion tempt us to rely totally on technical know-how at the risk of losing the wisdom of living that flows from vocal, mental, and contemplative prayer. Pressed by schedules too overloaded for our own good, we have no choice—or so it seems—but to skim across the surface of existence, never plumbing its depths. We approach life with a "fix it up and get on with it" mentality and miss the chance to advance in wisdom. We base our decisions on statistical averages and scoff at the lack of scientific evidence to support religious experiences. We value displays of human power while passing over the power of the Spirit.

Following the way of wisdom leads us to harmonize head and heart, calculation and contemplation. Instead of fretting over every failure, we try to heed Christ's counsel not to worry because "… can any of [us] by worrying add a single hour to [our] span of life?" (Luke 12:25). Anxiety decreases the moment attention to God's providential care increases. Living in faith, hope, and love restores our initiative to pursue excellence while avoiding fixation on functional accomplishment alone.

This back and forth rhythm of functionality and spirituality, of inspiration and incarnation, is indelibly intertwined in every Christian life. The Apostle Paul pleads with us "to lead a life worthy of the calling to which [we] have been called, with all humility and gentleness, with patience, bearing with one another in love, making every effort to maintain the unity of the Spirit in the bond of peace" (Ephesians 4:1-3).

In his *Spiritual Conferences*, the medieval Dominican preacher John Tauler (1300-1361) says in the same vein: "Do not go adopting other people's methods or spiritual exercises; that is blindness. Our various ways to God are as different from one another as we are ourselves. One man's spiritual meat is another man's poison, and the graces we are given vary in many ways, to fit the needs of our particular constitutions and natures. So leave other people's practices alone. Imitate their virtues, if you like: their humility, their gentleness and so on. But when it comes to external observances, follow your own particular vocation. Concentrate on knowing what you yourself are called to do, what God is asking of you and do that."[3]

We learn from Tauler that God conveys divine directives through the filter of seemingly unrelated circumstances, choices, and events. The richness of the ordinary constitutes the best arena in which to meet the challenge of remaining faithful to our calling in Christ.

LET US PRAY

Lord, grant me the flexibility to respond to the myriad demands and details of the day without losing track of their deeper meaning. Let me live in the conviction that they are conveyors of a mysterious invitation to discover ways of being and becoming I could never have anticipated. Keep me attuned to your will in what has gone before, and in what is yet to come in that heavenly sphere when every tear will be wiped away (Revelation 7:17). *Amen.*

✦❦❧✦

4. EXPERIENCING STEADFAST LOVE

Because God loves us as a mother loves her child, God wants us to care for one another.

Can a woman forget her nursing child, or show no compassion for the child of her womb? Even these may forget, yet I will not forget you. See, I have inscribed you on the palms of my hands; your walls are continually before me (Isaiah 49:15-16).

The terror that pervades the hearts of parents whose child goes missing points to the truth of this prophetic word: God's love for us is so good, so personal, that none of us will ever be numbered among those deemed worthless or forgotten. No more than a mother could push a nursing child away from her breast can God disregard our concerns. What a remarkable revelation it is that our name has been inscribed on the palm of God's hand and that our life in its minutest details is ever in God's sight.

This prophecy evokes a range of emotions from fear of unworthiness to faith in our having been chosen by God for a fruitful work no one else was destined to do. Such wide-ranging sentiments find a fitting place in this humble confession penned in the *Story of a Soul* by St. Thérèse of Lisieux (1873-1897):

> You know, Mother, I have always want-
> ed to be a saint. Alas! I have always noticed
> that when I compared myself to the saints,
> there is between them and me the same
> difference that exists between a mountain
> whose summit is lost in the clouds and the
> obscure grain of sand trampled underfoot
> by the passers-by. Instead of becoming
> discouraged, I said to myself: God cannot
> inspire unrealizable desires. I can then in
> spite of my littleness, aspire to holiness. It
> is impossible for me to grow up, and so I
> must bear with myself such as I am with all
> my imperfections. But I want to seek out a
> means of going to heaven by a little way,
> a way that is very straight, very short, and
> totally new.[4]

For St. Thérèse this "little way" can be summarized in one word: love. Like a perennial plant, it never fails to bloom. In a faithful heart like hers, the psalmist's prayer of praise comes to fruition: "O give thanks to the Lord, for he is good, for his steadfast love endures forever. O give thanks to the God of gods, for his steadfast love endures forever. O give thanks to the Lord of lords, for his steadfast love endures forever …" (Psalm 136:1-3).

Another master of the French School of spirituality with its emphasis on spiritual childhood was Jean-Pierre de Caussade (1695-1715). He writes in his masterpiece, *Abandonment to Divine Providence*: "So, dear souls, let us love, for love will give us everything. It gives us holiness and all that accompanies it. It is all around us and flows into every receptive heart. O what a thing is this holy seed which ripens into eternal life! We cannot praise it enough."[5]

Such love cannot confine itself to one locale; it is as ubiquitous as the air we breathe because "God is love" (1 John 4:16) and where love is, there God is to be found.

LET US PRAY

Lord, grant me the privilege of binding every facet of my temporal life to your eternal benevolence. Let all my actions reflect your unconditional, infinite love for souls and their harmonious unfolding. Allow me to radiate in childlike trust the light you enkindle from within when I hear and heed your word. May I strive to love others with the same love with which I have been loved. May charity be the hallmark of my appreciative heart, the harbor from where I set sail and the homeport to which I return. Amen.

❧·❦·❧

5.BECOMING MORE FAITHFUL
Fidelity is the endless symphony that binds our wayward being to the Trinity.

So we do not lose heart. Even though our outer nature is wast-

ing away, our inner nature is being renewed day by day. For this slight momentary affliction is preparing us for an eternal weight of glory beyond all measure, because we look not at what can be seen but at what cannot be seen; for what can be seen is temporary, but what cannot be seen is eternal (2 Corinthians 4:16-18).

The temptation from which we ask to be spared every time we say the "Our Father" is that of failing to pass the double test of fidelity and forgiveness. Failure seems to loom before us when we ignore the suffering of the innocent and do nothing to prevent the random results of violence. The displacement of generosity by cold-blooded greed harms us all. We need only to stand on any street corner to witness uncharitable acts in conflict with gestures of kindness. Faith lets us proclaim in the face of such forces that it is possible to conform to Christ and through him to turn cups of suffering into chalices of mercy. We believe, despite avalanches of doubt, that we shall see the glory of the Lord in the land of the living.

Such was the faith of Father Walter Ciszek, S.J. (1904-1984), who suffered imprisonment in a Soviet gulag for over twenty years under a false accusation of espionage. In his soul-searching masterpiece, *He Leadeth Me*, he writes:

> Ultimately, we come to expect God to accept *our* understanding of what his will ought to be and to help us fulfill *that*, instead of learning to see and accept his will in the real situations in which he places us daily … To predict what God's will is going to be, to rationalize what his will must be, is at once a work of human folly and yet the subtlest of all temptations. The plain

and simple truth is that his will is what he
actually wills to send us each day, in the
way of circumstances, places, people, and
problems. The trick is to learn to see that—
not just in theory, or not just occasionally
in a flash of insight granted by God's grace,
but every day. Each of us has no need to
wonder about what God's will must be for
us; his will for us is clearly revealed in every situation of every day, if only we could
learn to view all things as he sees and sends
them to us.[6]

To grow in fidelity we must learn to shift our attention
from an urge to control the mystery to a desire to celebrate
its always surprising manifestations. God's will is not meant
to conform to our intended outcomes. Hard as it may be to
believe, we must live in the conviction that no prayer will
ever go as unanswered.

What follows is renewed hope and a way of loving we
have not known before: "In this is love, not that we loved
God, but that he loved us, and sent his Son to be the atoning
sacrifice for our sins. Beloved, since God loved us so much,
we also ought to love one another. No one has ever seen
God, [but] if we love one another, God lives in us, and his
love is perfected in us" (1 John 4:10-12).

If the Father cares for a single sparrow, how much more
does he care for us? The countless blessings we receive from
God have to be returned to God by means of the love and
service we offer to others. The virtues of faith, hope, and
charity prove their efficacy in action, for deeds always speak
louder than words.

LET US PRAY

Lord, in obedience to your will, let me remain faithful to my daily duty. Lessen my resistance to do what must be done. To follow you prevents me from straying into egocentric traps that deflect me from your grand design for my life. Remind me, whenever I lose heart, that our Father in Heaven sees to it that everything works together for the good of those who love him and promise to keep his word. Give me the courage to say with the saints I seek to emulate, "Your will be done, though in my own undoing." Amen.

✦⇌⁂⇌✦

6. CHANGING OUR HEART
God hides in the hermitage of our heart.

Listen to me, O coastlands, pay attention you peoples from far away! The Lord called me before I was born, while I was in my mother's womb he named me. He made my mouth like a sharp sword, in the shadow of his hand he hid me; he made me a polished arrow, in his quiver he hid me away (Isaiah 49:1-2).

One point on which scripture and the masters agree is that, on the path to intimacy with God, what has to change is our heart. Until this depth of conversion occurs, we can neither renew our lives nor affect for the better the world around us. That which pleases God is not a litany of our accomplishments but the state of our heart. There is no place we can hide from the gaze of God since from the beginning "[our] life is hidden with Christ in God" (Colossians 3:3).

Carlo Carretto (1910-1988) confirms this truth: "So it is not by fleeing that you will find God more easily, but it is by changing your heart that you see things differently. The desert in the city is only possible on these terms: that you see things with a new eye, touch them with a new spirit, love them with a new heart."[7]

While it may not be impossible for us to go to the Sahara desert as Carretto did, we can retire at any time or place to the hermitage of our heart. This inner desert then becomes a living symbol of the integration of contemplation and action, which is the goal sought by anyone who promises to follow Jesus. When the burden of bearing his message gets the best of us, we can do as he did and go off to a quiet oasis, that is to say, we can retire to the desert of our heart and refresh ourselves in prayer.

In his book *Seeds of Hope*, Henri Nouwen (1932-1996) says, "Prayer is the way to both the heart of God and the heart of the world—precisely because they have been joined through the suffering of Jesus Christ … Praying is letting one's own heart become the place where the tears of God and the tears of God's children can merge and become tears of hope."[8]

Dorothy Day (1897-1980) makes an even bolder claim in her autobiography, *The Long Loneliness*: "If we love God with our whole hearts, how much heart have we left? If we love with our whole mind and soul, [how much] strength have we left? We must live this life now. Death changes nothing. If we do not learn to enjoy God now we never will. If we do not learn to praise him and thank him and rejoice in him now, we never will."[9]

LET US PRAY

Lord, in your mercy silence my excessive ambitions for worldly success and recognition divorced from dependence on you alone. Grant me the grace of experiencing harmony between my inmost longing for you and the immediate labors I must accomplish. Whenever my resolve weakens, fan the embers of courage I need to enflame the process of conversion, from initial consent to acceptance of the cross. Amen.

✦➤❧✦➤

7. FINDING TRUE HAPPINESS

True happiness resides in our total abandonment to the Beloved.

Happy are those who ... rejoice in your prosperity. Happy also are all people who grieve with you because of your afflictions; for they will rejoice with you and witness all your glory forever (Tobias 13:14).

The desire to pursue happiness is a goal implanted by God in each of our souls. The Decalogue in the Old Testament tells us what we must do to reach this goal; it requires giving priority first and foremost to not acting contrary to the law of God. The Sermon on the Mount in the New Testament is a mixture of commands and consolations that reveal the secrets of a happy life. These "attitudes of being" or "be-attitudes" are blessings pertinent to our life here-and-now; they also forecast the future God has in store for faithful souls.[10] What could make us happier than to be pure enough of heart to see God or to be poor enough in spirit to claim our humble place in the kingdom of God?

In *The Soul's Journey into God*, St. Bonaventure (c. 1217-1274) says, "Since happiness is nothing other than the enjoyment of the highest good and since the highest good is above, no one can be made happy unless he rise above himself, not by an ascent of the body, but of the heart."[11] The search for happiness is less about finding a self-proclaimed formula that fulfills our desires and more about trusting Christ to show us how to obey the Father's will in every situation.

The key to happiness is to keep our eyes focused on the highest good, to be unbound from the fetters of mere analytical reason and to fasten our glance on faith. We need two wings of truth—reason and faith—to find and fulfill our divine destiny.

Aelred of Rievaulx (1110-1167), a medieval Cistercian abbot and the author of *On Spiritual Friendship*, asks this insightful question about the experience of the blessed life: "Was it not a foretaste of blessedness thus to love and thus to be loved; thus to help and thus to be helped; and in this way from the sweetness of fraternal charity to wing one's flight aloft to that more sublime splendor of divine love, and by the ladder of charity now to mount to the embrace of Christ himself; and again to descend to the love of neighbor, there pleasantly to rest?"[12]

Being abandoned to God and feeling blessed are two branches of the vine of love Christ plants in our heart. As witnesses to the Good News, he wants us to say with unwavering conviction: "Happy are those who do not follow the advice of the wicked, or take the paths that sinners tread or sit in the seat of scoffers; but their delight is in the law of the Lord ... they are like trees planted by the stream of water, which yield their fruit in its season and their leaves do not wither" (Psalms 1:1-3).

LET US PRAY

Good Shepherd, though at times I may feel lost and forlorn, help me to return to the pasture of your presence. There and there alone does happiness reign supreme. Wrap me tightly in your outstretched arms and teach me how to become a disciple unafraid to proclaim your covenant of love to recalcitrant people. Satisfy my hunger and thirst to know the one God in Three Persons that you are. Amen.

PART TWO
SHARING OUR GIFTS
WITH ONE ANOTHER

✦❧➌❦➍

1. Freedom from Self-Seeking
2. Practicing the Presence of God
3. Growing in Compassion
4. Becoming "Little Words" in the Eternal Word
5. Living in Forgiveness
6. Proclaiming God's Power in Powerlessness
7. Remaining Resilient in the Face of Adversity

✦❧➌❦➍

1. FREEDOM FROM SELF-SEEKING

Every epiphany of the mystery is an invitation to be free from selfish acquisitions.

For while gentle silence enveloped all things, and night in its swift course was now half gone, your all-powerful word leapt from heaven, from the royal throne, into the midst of the land that was doomed, a stern warrior carrying the sharp sword of your authentic command, and stood and filled all things with death, and touched heaven while standing on the earth (Wisdom 18:14-16).

Self-seeking, combined with defensive excuses for bad behavior and an inability to be forgiving of self and others as God forgives us, is the surest sign of our fallen condition. The alternative Christian way begins with self-giving whereby we witness to the agapic outpouring of love that won our salvation. Our Savior leapt into our doomed world to announce the reconstitution of the earth and the heavenly destiny of its inhabitants. The "stern warrior" commanded us to rise from the dead fields of stubborn selfishness and turn in freedom to the life of righteousness he came to reveal.

This meeting of earth and heaven intrigued the medieval mystic Meister Eckhart (1260-1339). He expresses our need to ponder this restorative narrative in deep prayer and in the silence that is the "outcome of a quiet mind." He reiterates: "The quieter the mind, the more powerful, the worthier, the deeper, the more telling and more perfect the prayer is. To the quiet mind all things are possible. What is a quiet mind? A quiet mind is one which nothing weighs on, nothing worries, which, free from ties and from all self-seeking, is wholly merged into the will of God and dead to its own. Such a one can do no deed, however small, that is not clothed with something of God's power and authority. It behooves us to pray hard so that all our mortal members with their powers—eyes, ears, mouth and all their senses—are turned in that direction, and we must never stop until we find ourselves on the point of union with him we have in mind and are praying to, namely, God.[13]

On the obstacle-strewn path of freedom from self-seeking, it often feels as if we are making little or no progress. Like wind-tossed reeds along the riverbank of life, we are cast hither and yon by storms so fierce they threaten to flatten us to the ground. When the fury of Mother Nature subsides and we have the stamina to start again, we are amazed at the resilience fragile reeds like us display. There we are, held up by fortitude and perseverance, feeling like dried leaves tossed by every wind and yet refusing to lose heart.

Is it not because far below the surface of the ground, in silent depths, the tree has dug its roots into bedrock, where it finds the strength to be blown back and forth in the wind and to upright itself when the wind stops? And so must it be with us. When we fail, it is not a signal to fall apart but to present the whole of our bruised and broken being to God, saying, "Here I am." With the freedom given to us by God, we seek renewal. We give this body of ours, with its weaknesses and strengths; this intellect, with its confusion and clarity; this heart, with its hardness and pliability to the Beloved. To say, "Here I am," is to offer the Lord the trials and talents entrusted to us and to use them as teaching tools. Lessons learned in life's school of hard knocks ready us to follow our Master wherever he leads. Freed from self-seeking, we are better able to be his friends and faithful servants.

LET US PRAY

Lord, help me to be committed to my call to be at once free and bound. I have the duty to choose which way to go and yet I have but one desire: to conform to your will. Please protect me from the demons of selfishness that besiege me. Amidst the pressures of daily life, open the ears of my heart to hear your voice in the depths of my being. Let me see that the closer I come to you, the more I am able to say when you call, "Here I am." Amen.

✦➻❧➻✦

2. PRACTICING THE PRESENCE OF GOD
The hunger in our heart can never be satisfied until we experience lasting union with God.

...[Since] the one who is seated on the throne will shelter [us], [we] will hunger no more, and thirst no more; the sun will not

strike [us], nor any scorching heat; for the Lamb at the center of the throne will be [our] shepherd, and he will guide [us] to springs of the water of life, and God will wipe away every tear from [our] eyes (Revelation 7:15-17).

This awesome promise motivates us to practice the presence of God, not occasionally as in church on Sunday, not whimsically as when we do not feel well, but at all times under every circumstance.

Two spiritual masters confirm the efficacy of this practice. William Law (1686-1761) says in *A Serious Call to a Devout and Holy Life*, "There is nothing that so powerfully governs the heart, that so strongly excites us to wise and reasonable actions, as a true sense of God's presence."[14] Brother Lawrence of the Resurrection (1614-1691) adds in *The Practice of the Presence of God*, "There is no way of life in the world more agreeable or delightful than continual conversation with God; only those who practice and experience it can understand this. I do not suggest, however, that you do it for this reason. We must not seek consolations from this exercise, but must do it from a motive of love, and because God wants it. If I were a preacher, I would preach nothing but the practice of the presence of God; and if I were a spiritual director, I would recommend it to everyone, for I believe there is nothing so necessary or so easy."[15]

These insights confirm that the comings and goings of daily life are not haphazard events but messengers of the Mystery. Each of them represents an opportunity, allowed by God, to help us perfect this holy practice. It is our responsibility to disclose the hidden meaning each happening harbors. From conception to death, we are in a process of being formed, reformed, and transformed by the power of the Holy Spirit. This gift of grace is not meant for our own edification only; we are to share it with abandoned souls in every walk of life.

When the practice of the presence of God and the peace it grants pervades our life and world, we are more attuned to the meaning of unplanned and unwanted changes. With the Apostle Paul, we feel emboldened enough to say: "Rejoice in the Lord always; again I will say, Rejoice. Let your gentleness be known to everyone. The Lord is near. Do not worry about anything, but in everything by prayer and supplication with thanksgiving let your requests be made known to God. And the peace of God which surpasses all understanding, will guard your hearts and minds in Christ Jesus" (Philippians 4:4-7).

LET US PRAY

Lord, make me appreciate that everyday life is a commingling of the familiar and the unexpected. In the course of appraising the meaning of what I experience from a biblical perspective, keep me attuned to the guiding presence of the Holy Spirit. Let me never derail the processes of formation, reformation, and transformation initiated by your "tender mercy ... [guiding] our feet into the way of peace" (Luke 1:78-79). Amen.

✦•❧❦•✦

3. GROWING IN COMPASSION
In the mirror of our compassion others see the face of Christ.

The compassion of human beings is for their neighbors, but the compassion of the Lord is for every living thing. He rebukes and trains and teaches them, and turns them back, as a shepherd his flock. He has compassion on those who accept his discipline and who are eager for his precepts (Sirach 18:13-14).

Compassion enables us to behold behind a façade of external failings the infinite dignity and worth of each person. It reminds us, despite our differences, of the likeness we share as members of the same human family. The best exchanges between us, from enjoying tea and toast to engaging in spiritual direction, ought to be as full of passion as of compassion. We encourage one another to be our best selves. We laugh and cry together, rejoicing at our good fortune and lamenting our losses. We sense how alike we really are. No matter what status of life we have attained, our flesh burns when it touches flame. However brilliant or limited our minds may be, we try to activate the gifts and talents we've received. At a podium fit for a professor or in a wheelchair that has become the legs we lost, we operate from the perspective of what it means to be fully human. Compassion so affects our character that we never ignore the pleas for help we hear.

The Quaker writer Thomas R. Kelly (1893-1941) reminds us in his *Testament of Devotion* that "We cannot keep the love of God to ourselves. It spills over. It quickens us. It makes us see the world's needs anew. We love people and we grieve to see them blind when they think they might be seeing, asleep with all the world's comforts when they ought to be awake and living sacrificially, accepting the world's goods as their right when they really hold them only in temporary trust. It is because from this holy Center we relove people, relove our neighbors as ourselves, that we are bestirred to be means of their awakening."[16]

The virtue that warms us like a homey hearth in an often cold and cruel world is compassion. The moment we place our healing hands on the shoulders of a suffering other, we feel ourselves to be in the presence of the Divine

Healer without whose help our best efforts may bear little or no lasting fruit. The invitation Jesus issues is one we
ought to accept: "Abide in me as I abide in you. Much as
the branch cannot bear fruit by itself unless it abides in the
vine, neither can you unless you abide in me. I am the vine,
you are the branches. Those who abide in me and I in them
bear much fruit, because apart from me you can do nothing" (John 15:4-5).

Each time we treat another "branch" of this eternal
"vine" with compassion, we know what it is to receive far
more than we could ever give. We extend the credit others
offer us to the Divine Giver we serve. It humbles us to know
that Christ chooses us to be his voice, his hands, his healers
in the hospitals of daily life. Each expression of compassion
points to our own and others' vulnerability. Fragile though
we are, we go forth unafraid, confident that the Lord is near
and that he has commanded us to show mercy in his name.

LET US PRAY

*Lord, deadening forces of merciless treatment can never bear
up under the weight of your compassion. One gesture of mercy
can outweigh a history of mistreatment. To mature in discipleship
is to become an instrument in the symphony of life you conduct
every day. The more I abide with you, the more able I am to convey to others the mercy I have received from you so undeservedly.
From the finest hospice to the poorest hovel, you are there. Endless
are the reaches of your compassionate care for sick souls in need of
healing. Amen.*

✦✦✦

4. BECOMING "LITTLE WORDS" IN THE ETERNAL WORD

The Word of God is alive in every longing heart.

Indeed, the Word of God is living and active, sharper than any two-edged sword, piercing until it divides soul from spirit, joints from marrow; it is able to judge the thoughts and intentions of the heart (Hebrews 4:12).

We may feel as if there is never enough time in the day to devote to slowed-down, dwelling, meditative reading, but is that really true? Can we not find twenty minutes or so, in even the busiest day, to let go of our attachment to clock time and place ourselves in the presence of God's word? Needy pilgrims like us can never take for granted the fact that the Holy Spirit can and does use the power of sacred words to touch and transform our lives. To turn to the Bible or the text of a spiritual master is not the privilege of monks or nuns only but a practice for all believers and sincere seekers. The wisdom contained therein helps us to see that nothing happens without its being guided by God's providential plan for our lives. In all persons, events and things, we encounter Jesus Christ, the eternal self-expression of the Father whose living Word draws us into the heart of salvation history.

As St. John of the Cross (1542-1591) says so eloquently in his *Sayings of Light and Love*, "The Father spoke one Word, which was his Son, and this Word he speaks in eternal silence, and in silence must it be heard by the soul."[17] The art of formative reading invites us to practice the discipline of silent adoration. Only then can we hear the still, unassuming whispers of the Holy Spirit and interpret what they mean.

In the Letter to the Hebrews, the importance of listening

takes on a special urgency: "Take care, brothers and sisters, that none of you may have an evil, unbelieving heart that turns away from the living God. But exhort one another every day, as long as it is called 'today,' so that none of you may be hardened by the deceitfulness of sin. For we have become partners of Christ, if only we hold our first confidence firm to the end. As it is said, 'Today, if you hear his voice, do not harden your hearts …'" (Hebrews 3:12-15).

To be "little words" in the Eternal Word is a lifelong process. It starts when we let go of our own agendas and cooperate with the grace of renewal we must undergo—until at last God becomes our all in All.

LET US PRAY

Lord, in your mercy block the flood of selfish words that threaten to inundate the word you want me to hear. Before I can put my life wholly in your hands, I need your words to be etched on my heart. Any time I feel incapable of doing so, lift the little word I am into your light and grant me the supernatural strength to be faithful to your Eternal Word. Remind me of the simple truth that there is nothing I can do on my own and that without your help a lasting sense of purpose will always elude me. Amen.

✛❧✛❧

5. LIVING IN FORGIVENESS

Forgiveness only makes sense when we stand with open arms at the foot of the cross.

Put away from you all the bitterness and wrath and anger and wrangling and slander, together with all malice, and be kind to one another, tender-hearted, forgiving one another, as God in Christ has forgiven you (Ephesians 4:31-32).

Behold the cross. Like a brand burned on the tissue of each believer's heart is the truth that as Christ forgave us, so must we forgive one another. This love of the cross drew St. Elizabeth of the Trinity (1880-1906) to say in her *Complete Works*: "The soul that wants to serve God day and night in His temple—I mean this inner sanctuary of which St. Paul speaks when he says, 'The temple of God is holy and you are that temple,' this soul must be resolved to share *fully* in its Master's passion. It is one of the redeemed who in its turn must redeem other souls, and for that reason it will sing on its lyre: 'I glory in the cross of Jesus Christ.' 'With Christ I am nailed to the cross …' And again, 'I suffer in my body what is lacking in the passion of Christ for the sake of his body, which is the Church.'"[18]

Those of us who, like St. Elizabeth, have suffered ailments of body and soul may have the courage to bring these experiences to prayer and thus to receive the grace of avoiding self-pity and blaming God or others for our misfortune. Forgiveness is the anecdote for the poison of bitterness. It allows us to see suffering as a blessing in disguise because of the purifying effect it has on our whole being. There is no better way to bring the process of inner purification to its destined end than to forgive others as God has forgiven us.

In due time we may be granted the freedom that comes when we do our best to forget the hurts inflicted on us. To both forgive and forget awakens us from illusions of perfection on our own and others' part. Anger can erupt into violence; hatred can replace love; envy can kill originality. These sins serve to remind us that no offense, great as it may be, can block the flow of divine forgiveness: "But they and our ancestors presumptuously stiffened their necks and did not obey your commandments; they refused to obey, and were not mindful of the wonders that you performed among them; but they stiffened their necks and determined to return to their slavery in Egypt. But you are a God ready to forgive, gracious and merciful, slow to anger and abounding in steadfast love, and you did not forsake them" (Nehemiah 9:16-17).

Forgiveness removes the inner and outer blockages that prevent us from growing in self-forgetful love. Everyone benefits when we pass this gift from person to person, forgiving one another as we have been forgiven by God.

LET US PRAY

Lord, no amount of gratitude can match the transformation granted to me through the gift of forgiveness. Teach me by your example never to return evil for evil and always to forgive those who sin against me. Let forgiveness become second nature to me so that I may banish every temptation to withhold its healing power and perpetuate what is evil in your sight. Amen.

✦◦❖◦✦

6. PROCLAIMING GOD'S POWER IN POWERLESSNESS

Powerlessness readies us to accept the power that flows forth from the cross.

When I came to you, brothers and sisters, I did not come proclaiming the mystery of God to you in lofty words or wisdom. For I decided to know nothing among you except Jesus Christ, and him crucified. And I came to you in weakness and in fear and in much trembling. My speech and my proclamation were not with plausible words of wisdom, but with a demonstration of the Spirit and of power, so that your faith might rest not on human wisdom but on the power of God (1 Corinthians 2:1-5).

Strength in weakness is a paradox we may find difficult to grasp. It is beyond the realm of reason to attribute the power to save the world to an instrument of torture like the cross, yet that is the truth our faith teaches. The Savior of the world began his mission not as a widely proclaimed ruler bedecked with embroidered robes or as a soldier commanding an army, but as a vulnerable baby in Bethlehem. In him, the impossible became possible.

Even a man as gifted as St. Augustine of Hippo (354-430) could not bring himself to believe in Jesus Christ until the hammer of divine grace broke open his heart. Only then did he realize how much he might have missed had he not resolved the riddle of strength in weakness. In his *Confessions* he cries: "Too late have I loved you, O Beauty so ancient and so new, too late have I loved you! Behold, you were within me, while I was outside: it was there that I sought you, and, a deformed creature, rushed headlong upon these things of beauty which you have made. You were with me, but I was not with you. They kept me far from you, those fair things which, if they were not in you, would not exist at all. You have called to me, and have cried out, and have shattered my deafness. You have blazed forth with light, and have shone upon me, and you have put my blindness to flight! You have sent forth fragrance, and I have drawn in my breath, and I pant after you. I have tasted you, and I hunger and thirst after you. You have touched me, and I have burned for your peace."[19]

For all his powers as a philosopher and teacher, St. Augustine had looked for God in the wrong places. In the process he overlooked the truth that in the beauty of this world, in the first revelation in creation, we behold the glory of God:

The heavens are telling the glory of God;
and the firmament proclaims his handiwork.
Day to day pours forth speech, and night to night
    declares knowledge.
There is no speech, nor are there words;
their voice is not heard;
yet their voice goes out through all the earth,
and their words to the end of the world (Psalms 19:1-4).

The first and most essential force of discipleship, as St. Augustine learned after his conversion, is humility. To push our own ego to the front lines of success, forgetful of God, is a formula for failure. Unless we acknowledge our nothingness, we cannot proclaim God's allness nor abide by the truth that whatever we do is God's doing in and through us.

LET US PRAY

Lord, help me in the night of faith to rely on the illuminating power of your crucified and risen glory. In painful moments of loneliness, doubt, and misunderstanding, reveal to me anew what you sacrificed for my sake. Each moment I spend in adoration of the cross offers me an opportunity to share in your Paschal Mystery. Inspire me to venerate in the disfigured faces of the poor, the underprivileged, the sick, and the maimed, the lame and the lonely, your hidden face as the Lamb of God, martyred in and with them for the salvation of the world. Amen.

7. REMAINING RESILIENT IN THE FACE OF ADVERSITY

Adversity is the soil in which joyful resilience abounds.

My brothers and sisters, whenever you face trials of any kind, con-

sider it nothing but joy, because you know that testing of your faith produces endurance, and let endurance have its full effect, so that you may be mature and complete, lacking in nothing (James 1:2-4).

Affliction puts before us two choices. It can convince us that God does not love us or it can lead us to new depths of appreciative abandonment to the Mystery. Wounded, weary souls like ours only find rest at the foot of the cross. The battlefield in our heart flows over like hot lava into the world. Love would cool its heat but instead hatred often abounds. What is wild and irrational replaces what is calm and ordered by God. Old wounds become open sores and pain destroys our peace.

Such affliction could annihilate hope were it not for the fact that Christ chose the cross as the only means to eradicate evil and to let us see on Easter morn the triumph of the good.

In his *Letters and Papers from Prison,* the Lutheran theologian Dietrich Bonhoeffer (1906-1945), penned this most resilient of prayers, knowing that he would soon have to face the execution squad:

> *O Lord my God, thank you for bringing this day*
>   *to a close;*
> *Thank you for giving me rest in body and soul.*
> *Your hand has been over me and has guarded and*
>   *preserved me.*
> *Forgive my lack of faith and any wrong that I have done*
> *today, and help me to forgive all who have wronged me…*
> *O God, your holy name be praised. Amen.* [20]

Faith drew Bonhoeffer from the confinement of a prison cell to a space of grace from which he beheld in his mind's eye the light and power of the Risen Lord. He interpreted the adversity of tortuous incarceration as the only way to conquer vice and excel in virtue.

In the same vein, Adrian van Kaam (1920-2007) says in *The Roots of Christian Joy*, "At times we may be touched by the gentle outpouring of eternal generosity in myriad wondrous forms of creation. It may happen to us while walking under majestic trees, catching the smile of a child, savoring the mellow colors softly painted by the Fall, delighting in the salty ocean breeze, watering a blossoming plant on our window sill, or looking in wonder at the miracles of nature brought nearer to us by art and science ... we may be imbued with the light of resilient joy when life becomes a nightmare of sorrow, loss and failure. Pain and disappointment, illness and death may be appraised in faith as another announcement of the coming of the kingdom. We may be infused with the joy-filled sadness of Jesus, reminding us gently of the grain that has to die before it may yield fruit."[21]

The English mystic Julian of Norwich (c. 1342-1423), who received special revelations concerning the meaning of the cross, said in her *Showings*: "... the whole reason why we pray is to be united into the vision and contemplation of him to whom we pray, wonderfully rejoicing with reverent fear, and with so much sweetness and delight in him that we cannot pray at all except as he moves us at the time."[22] Julian saw us as a besieged and broken people, succumbing to sin and having to suffer its consequences. To her such sickness of soul was cured by perfect love and the promise of wellness granted to her by the Lord.

LET US PRAY

Lord, when misery mutes my desire for intimacy with you, remind me to focus anew on the details of the day in which you reveal your loving plan for all people. Draw me from the blindness of sin to the bracing peaks of salvation history. In times of trial and terror, free me from entrapment in this valley of tears and console me with the truth that when I feel most troubled, that is when you are most near. Amen.

PART THREE
LISTENING TO THE BELOVED

✦❦❧❦✦

1. Living in Humility
2. Lifted to New Levels of Spiritual Awakening
3. Denying Ourselves to Follow Jesus
4. Moving from Desolation to Consolation
5. Enjoying the Fruits of Discipleship
6. Being Attuned to the Pace of God's Grace
7. Becoming Living Prayer

✦❦❧❦✦

1. LIVING IN HUMILITY

Seeing our limits as blessings opens our hearts to the grace of humility.

My child, perform your tasks with humility; then you will be loved by those whom God accepts. The greater you are, the more you must humble yourself; so you will find favor in the sight of the Lord. For great is the might of the Lord; but by the humble he is glorified (Sirach 3:17-20).

Without humility, Christian maturity remains an elusive goal. The option to "ease God out" (EGO) makes a mockery of our interior life. It separates us from the truth that we are nothing and that God is all.

Stubborn pride also has a bad effect on family relationships. The poison of pride can be seen in parents abusing children, in siblings at one another's throat, in mistakes never forgiven. Healing only begins with the humble admission that we are all sinners in need of redemption.

People puffed up by pride may find it hard to believe that God exalts the lowly. That is why St. Benedict of Nursia (480-550) wrote in his *Rule*, "The first step of humility is un-hesitating obedience, which comes naturally to those who cherish Christ above all."[23] Living in a posture of humble lis-tening is a grace we receive, not a virtue we can put on and take off at will. When we listen to God, the answer may not meet our vain predictions, but only the truth that is humility can ready us for the lessons God wants us to learn.

The first is that suffering—and the quest for meaning it evokes—moves us out of the range of our control. It may seem impossible to endure the trials obedience to the Gos-pel demands of us, but we need not worry if only we live in humility. It teaches us to wait for help, confident that God will not test us beyond our strength to endure.

In his meditation on *The Soul's Journey into God*, St. Bonaventure says: "Whoever wishes to ascend to God must first avoid sin, which deforms our nature, then exercise his natural powers … by praying, to receive restoring grace; by a good life, to receive purifying justice; by meditating, to receive illuminating knowledge; and by contemplating, to receive perfecting wisdom."[24]

Aided by the example of Jesus who humbled himself for our sake (Philippians 2:3-8), we can embrace our limits and celebrate them as blessings in disguise. The wisdom that we gain through suffering confirms that God "gives grace to the humble" (1 Peter 5:5). This virtue above all sustains us in body, mind, and spirit.

As we read in Isaiah 30:15, "By waiting and by calm you shall be saved, in quiet and in trust your strength lies." Jesus is the still point in the midst of our turning world. He invites us to find our strength by investing all that we are and do in humble trust of him. In an "up and at it," 24/7 culture, the loudest voices seem to exude the most power. A truly strong person, however, manifests humility and behaves with patience and perseverance.

LET US PRAY

Lord, show me that when I follow you in humility I am on the way to ascending the heights of transforming love. Maintaining a humble heart endows my humanity with confident faith, gentle peace, and a gracious demeanor. In the humus *of daily life, let the* humor *of my finitude fill me anew with the grace of* humility. *May my life on earth be and become an epiphany of your Mystery, forming, reforming, and transforming every facet of this wayward world. Amen.*

❧❦❧

2.   LIFTED TO NEW LEVELS OF SPIRITUAL AWAKENING
Grace lifts us to levels of spiritual awakening beyond imagining.

The fear of the Lord is the crown of wisdom, making peace and perfect health to flourish. She rained down knowledge and discerning comprehension, and she heightened the glory of those who held fast. To fear the Lord is the root of wisdom, and her branches are long life (Sirach 1:18-20).

Awe, or holy fear, is the beginning of wisdom since no amount of reasoning alone can exhaust the mystery of life and death, of cosmic wonders constantly being discovered, of the ultimate unknowability of God's immanence and transcendence. Little wonder we shake our heads and ask with the psalmist: "What are human beings that you are mindful of them, mortals that you care for them"? (Psalm 8:4).

Søren Kierkegaard (1813-1855), a renowned philosopher and an uncompromising Christian, places his understanding of fear of the Lord in the form of the following petitionary prayer: "Lord Jesus Christ, let Thy Holy Spirit enlighten our minds and convince us thoroughly of our sin, so that, humbled and with downcast eyes, we may recognize that we stand far, far off and with a sigh, 'God be merciful to me a sinner'; but then let it befall us by Thy grace as it befell that publican who went up to the Temple to pray and went down to his house justified."[25]

The gift of spiritual awakening, be it fleeting or prolonged, invites us to find the bridge between the fragility of our existence and the dispensation of God's mercy. A plane crashes. A drive-by shooting occurs. An earthquake kills hundreds of innocent people. Why were some spared and not others? There is no easy answer to these soul-searching questions. We either maintain faith in God's unconditional embrace or we consign ourselves and others to the fickleness of fate. When people are treated unjustly, we do not stand by, indifferent to their plight. We enter into what they are feeling and try to help them as much as we can. When they are bent under the weight of worry, we do not turn a blind eye, but share their burden.

This combination of an enlightened mind and a compassionate heart is a sure sign that grace has elevated us to new levels of spiritual maturity. In prayer and presence to the Lord, we see with the psalmist the wonder that awaits us: "You prepare a table before me in the presence of my enemies; you anoint me with oil; my cup overflows. Surely goodness and mercy shall follow me all the days of my life, and I shall dwell in the house of the Lord my whole life long" (Psalm 23:5-6).

The stormy crossings of life fade from memory the moment we come home to the Lord. We laugh at those foolish moments when we distrusted God's goodness or expected instant returns for the smallest gesture of good will on our part. Forgetfulness of our destiny ends, and the dawning of its pursuit begins anew, as soon as we reconfirm who we are as friends and followers of Jesus.

LET US PRAY

Lord, give me the courage both to "go beyond" and to "go more deeply into" all that transpires during my sojourn on earth. Keep me open to the horizon of transcendent truth that lies beyond sensual gratification and functional satisfaction. Dissolve the illusion that the fulfillment of worldly desires is enough to satisfy my deepest longings. Draw me daily into new depths of spiritual awareness and new heights of surrender to you. Amen.

3. DENYING OURSELVES TO FOLLOW JESUS

The Holy Spirit implants in our soul the "yes" of the Son to the will of the Father.

He came out and went, as was his custom, to the Mount of Olives; and the disciples followed him. When he reached the place, he said to them, "Pray that you may not come into the time of trial." Then he withdrew from them about a stone's throw, knelt down, and prayed, "Father, if you are willing, remove this cup from me; yet not my will but yours be done." Then an angel from heaven appeared to him and gave him strength (Luke 22:39-43).

Many are the times in life when, we, too, pray for the strength to surrender to the Father's will as Jesus did. We enter our own gardens of Gethsemane anxious but unafraid, curious what will happen but convinced that we are not alone. God's grace sustains and surrounds us. It prompts us to renew our faith in the cross because its apparent finality marked the beginning of our redemption by the risen Lord.

The light of Christ's glory, like the sun, shines equally on everyone. We can hide from its radiance in the shadowy wood of sin, or allow it to guide us to the path of repentance where we can start our life's journey anew. Once we say yes to the Father as Jesus did, there is no need to fear the unknown.

The medieval monk William of St. Thierry (c. 1080- c. 1148) relates in his *Golden Epistle* the meaning of surrender to a mystery we may never fathom but that we can affirm. In a letter addressed to his brothers at the monastery of Mount Dieu he says: "... this way of thinking about God does not lie at the disposal of the thinker. It is a gift of grace, bestowed by the Holy Spirit who breathes where he chooses, when he chooses, how he chooses and upon whom he chooses. Man's part is continually to prepare his heart by ridding his will of foreign attachments, his reason or intellect of anxieties, his memory of idle or absorbing ... business, so that in the Lord's good time and when he sees fit, at the sound of the Holy Spirit's breathing the elements which constitute thought may be free at once to come together and do their work, each contributing its share to the outcome of joy for the soul. The will displays pure affection for the joy which the Lord gives, the memory yields faithful material, the intellect affords the sweetness of experience."[26]

Just as the only way out of a dilemma is the way through

it, so there is no shortcut to "ridding our will of foreign attachments." We either drink from the chalice of other-centered love or foolishly push it aside. Our poor choice does
not diminish the riches that remain in the cup. They are
there for us when we are humble enough to receive them.
What was once distasteful to us may now be delectable.

The lesson we learn through surrender to our crucified
and risen Lord is to welcome affliction as the road to spiritual freedom. No progress on this road is possible unless we
are willing to follow the master from Golgatha to the empty
tomb on Easter morn.

The Flemish mystic Hadewijch (c. 1200) concludes:
"For your part be vigilant and discerning in what you are
doing, attentive to yourselves and your quest, and firm in
your faith. Provided you seek in truth—following not your
emotional attraction but God's will—you shall obtain everything for which, in his love, [God] has destined you … If two
things are to become one, nothing may be between them except the glue wherewith they are united together. That bond
of glue is Love, whereby God and the blessed soul are united in oneness."[27]The bond of which Hadewijch speaks seals
off the barbs of self-centeredness that threatened to pierce
our heart. This "lofty surrender" enables us to stand before
the Lord, stripped of all illusion and ready at last to "cast
away all things for the sake of love."[28]

LET US PRAY

*Lord, thank you for strengthening the bedrock of my belief
that Christ conquered death to arouse my hope in life eternal. In
the radiant light of Easter morn, all of us have been transformed
in spirit, heart, mind, and will. Thank you for the gift of faith that
holds firm in the darkest of nights, revealing anew that I am not
in charge now—nor shall I ever be—of my own destiny. Teach*

me that the trials of life, painful as they may be, are instruments used by you to take me to a new place of grace in intimacy with the Trinity. Amen.

4. MOVING FROM DESOLATION TO CONSOLATION

The farther away God seems, the nearer God is to hearts who seek him without ceasing.

All this has come upon us, yet we have not forgotten you, or been false to your covenant. Our heart has not turned back, nor have our steps departed from your way, yet you have broken us in the haunt of jackals, and covered us with deep darkness (Psalm 44:17-19).

Devastating as the desert moments of our life may be, they have a purpose in God's plan. They compel us to go into what St. Catherine of Siena names the "cell of self-knowledge." Alone, with our support systems at their lowest ebb, we can hide neither from ourselves nor from God. In silence so deep no word but the Lord's can penetrate it, we have no choice but to listen to what God has to say about the providential direction of our life. It is humiliating to know that we are not in charge of its unfolding. We feel fragile and out of control, but nothing we accomplish can surpass this supernatural learning experience. Aridity encourages waiting upon the Lord without the illusion of predictable outcomes. Now is the time to assess in naked faith God's plan for our life. Now is the time to beg for the courage to put selfish sensuality aside and pursue our calling in the Lord.

The following prayer to his good friend, penned so humbly by St Gregory the Great (540-604) in his *Pastoral Care*, is one we all understand: "But in the shipwreck of this life, sustain me, I beseech you, with the plank of your prayers, so that, as my weight is sinking down, you may uplift me with your meritorious hand."[29]

When these shipwrecks overtake us, and before any sign of rescue reveals itself, we feel as if we have been flung on a desert island with no resources to sustain us. It is then that we may turn to a mystic like St. John of the Cross (1542-1591), who assures us that in these nights of faith, when all support seems to be lost, there occurs a union between the lover and the Beloved that is beyond all imagining. As he says in *The Spiritual Canticle*: "… however elevated God's communications and the experiences of his presence are, and however sublime a person's knowledge of him may be, these are not God essentially, nor are they comparable to him because, indeed, he is still hidden to the soul. Hence, regardless of all these lofty experiences, a person should think of him as hidden and seek him as one who is hidden …"[30]

This *via negativa* (the way of negation) suspends our ability to understand God's ways with us. It brings us to the point of knowing in love that faith alone sustains us. The *via affirmativa* (the way of affirmation) reveals that the felt absence of God is in reality the best proof of God's presence. How apt is the comparison between the soul in desolation and the man, Job, who represents this paradoxical moment perfectly when he laments, "If he comes to me I shall not see him, and if he goes away I shall not understand" (Job 9:11).

Given the paradox of presence in seeming absence, it is no wonder we walk by faith and not by sight. We anticipate the light of dawn after the darkness of the night. The Holy Spirit reminds us in this moment of truth that death itself is but a brief passage to eternal life. What is hidden from us now shall one day be disclosed in a trumpet blast of glory.

LET US PRAY

Lord, whether I am in a desert or on a mountaintop, I sense that the revelation of your coming to me cannot be denied. You empower me to meet you in times of sorrow and joy. Amidst setbacks and in the wonder of new starts, you release my potency for inner and outer renewal. These purifying, illuminating, and unifying experiences save me from the deadening effects of feeling abandoned by the mystery. May the love of Father, Son, and Holy Spirit soften all hardness of heart and show me how efficacious it is lose myself in your embrace. Amen.

✦⟫✦⟪✦

5. ENJOYING THE FRUITS OF DISCIPLESHIP

The more we efface ourselves, the more room there is for the light of the Lord to shine through us.

Every generous act of giving, with every perfect gift, is from above, coming down from the Father of lights, with whom there is no variation or shadow due to change. In fulfillment of his own purpose he gave us birth by the word of truth, so that we would become a kind of first fruits of his creatures (James 1:17-18).

Many acts of generosity validate the transformation described by the Apostle James, but only the redemptive love of Jesus can draw us away from self-indulgence and into the depths of discipleship. The reason we can love God with our whole being and serve our neighbors for God's sake is because we do not do so alone. God's love enables us to overcome evil with good. Divine Providence goes ahead of us to prepare the way we are to follow. In the domain of daily drudgery, in the drabness of the mundane, we do not lose heart. When we least expect it, we may be granted by grace moments of unspeakable gladness. In what seemed to be a never-ending struggle with conflicting calls, we receive a clear sign of our direction. The fog of frustration passes and we perceive how to fulfill God's plan. This seeing is God's gift to us. It is a knowing in unknowing that dispels all doubt and makes us more eager than ever to walk in the footsteps of the Lord.

A man who came to understand the meaning of self-knowledge through suffering love is Dietrich Bonhoeffer (1906-1945), author of *The Cost of Discipleship*. He writes from the depths of his experience of imprisonment by the Nazis and eventual martyrdom: "… Jesus invites all who travail and are heavy laden to throw off their own yoke and take his yoke upon them—and his yoke is easy, and his burden is light."[31]

To live in fidelity to Christ under the sign of the cross was for a man like Dietrich not an occasion for misery but a gift of mercy, offering peace for his soul and its highest joy. He was ready to pay the ultimate price, knowing that the time of adherence to state-run laws, and the compromises they demanded, was over. He was now under the yoke of the Lord, who knew the state of his heart and walked with him to the wall of execution. What he found under its shadow was not servile fear but a reunion with the Savior he had always loved and served. To follow him from grave to glory was a price he was more than willing to pay.

LET US PRAY

Lord, help me to discern those habits of disobedience and complacency that cause me to resist the pace of grace. Experience tells me that they are more tenacious than I may think. My heart can harden like a crater filled with the cement of sin. Open it in obedience to the inner voice that beckons me to let go of whatever prevents me from following you. Let me kneel before your altar and pray: "Purge me with hyssop, and I shall be clean; wash me, and I shall be whiter than snow" (Psalm 51:7). *Dissolve, as only you can, the last remnants of my resistance to grace. Disclose to me in humility the depth of my dependence on you. Let love of your cross be the surest sign of my release from this valley of death; let it restore my vision of new life. Amen.*

✦•✦✦✦•✦

6. BEING ATTUNED TO THE PACE OF GOD'S GRACE

The secret of staying with grace is to remember that love unending has already given us the grace to do so.

Now may our God and Father himself and our Lord Jesus direct our way to you. And may the Lord make you increase and abound in love for one another and for all, just as we abound in love for you. And may he so strengthen your hearts in holiness that you may be blameless before our God and Father at the coming of our Lord Jesus with all his saints (1 Thessalonians 3:11-13).

To be holy and blameless in the sight of God is not a goal we reach but a call to which we respond. This love relationship arouses in us a thirst for the transcendent, but what is that in comparison to God's thirst for us?

The invitation of grace is both appealing and challenging. Imagine the Most High as the conductor of a cosmic symphony that defies description. Each finely calibrated instrument plays its designated tune. At first faintly and then with full attention, we hear the music of eternity resonating in each temporal event. The inflowing and outflowing of grace match the rhythm of divine redemption and human longing and press words to the boundary of articulation.

Pseudo-Dionysius (c. 500), mystic and spiritual master, says: "For one must accept the truth of what scripture says: 'Eye has not seen and ear has not heard and it has not come to the heart of man what God has prepared for those who love him.' The bosom of the blessed patriarchs and of all the other saints signifies, I believe, this divine inheritance and this perfect beatitude where all those who have lived in conformity with God are welcomed into the ever-renewed perfection of unaging blessedness."[32]

To stay attuned to this "divine inheritance," we must defer to the guidance of God and strive to live in conformity to the grace we receive. No instrument in an orchestra operates on its own. All respond to the conductor, who draws a diversity of sound into one glorious symphony. In the same way, God grants each of us the grace we need to grow into the "ever-renewed perfection of unaging blessedness."

LET US PRAY

Lord, in cooperation with your grace, may I be as attentive to the benevolent guidance of the Holy Spirit as musicians are to the baton of their conductor. When heart responds to Heart, beauty and order bind together sense and spirit. What is finite and temporal bows to the mystery of what is infinite and eternal. The misery of dissonance gives way to the consonance of mercy. The action of grace makes of my being a living prayer: Beloved, be present in every decision and action that influences the unfinished symphony being played in the time allotted to me. Amen.

7. BECOMING LIVING PRAYER

Living prayer is the practice of ceaseless communion with God who dwells within us.

I do not cease to give thanks for you as I remember you in my prayers. I pray that the God of our Lord Jesus Christ, the Father of glory, may give you a spirit of wisdom and revelation as you come to know him, so that, with the eyes of your heart enlightened, you may know what is the hope to which he has called you, what are the riches of his glorious inheritance among the saints, and what is the immeasurable greatness of his power for us who believe, according to the working of his great power (Ephesians 1:16-19).

Holy Scripture changes our perception of who we are and why we are here. It teaches us to transform the world into the house of God. Worthwhile efforts serve this aim, provided we act in response to prayer and with reliance on grace. Living in faith, hope, and love, as described by the Apostle Paul, prevents us from erecting barriers between ourselves and God. Doors once closed to the mystery now open wide. Love once meted out in stingy dribbles now extends to the least of these. The deadening effects of living only for ourselves end and we become the fully alive people God intended us to be.

A saint and martyr, Edith Stein (1891-1942) chose the path of ceaseless prayer and unshakeable trust in God's providence. There was no way for her to escape the vicious intentions of her Nazi captors, but she was free to live by the truth she had found in her Carmelite vocation: "In other words, what did not lie in *my* plan lay in *God's* plan. And the more often such things happen to me the more lively becomes in me the conviction of my faith that—from God's point of view—nothing is *accidental*, that my entire life, even in the most minute details, was pre-designed in the plans of divine providence and is thus for the all-seeing eye of God a perfect coherence of meaning ... Once I begin to realize this, my heart rejoices in anticipation of the light of glory in whose sheen this coherence of meaning will be fully unveiled to me."[33]

This contemporary martyr understood what the Gestapo could not grasp, that when the Christ in one praying soul beholds the Christ in another, a bond of love forms between them that no act of violence, however heinous, can erase. Edith Stein (today known as St. Teresa Benedicta of the Cross) would have understood what another saint, Clare of Assisi (c. 1193-1254), experienced when she beheld her Beloved and clung to him with all her heart, saying he is the one Whose beauty all the heavenly hosts admire unceasingly,

Whose love inflames our love,
Whose contemplation is our refreshment,
Whose graciousness is our joy,
Whose gentleness fills us to overflowing,
Whose remembrance brings a gentle light,
Whose fragrance will revive the dead,
Whose glorious vision will be the happiness of all citizens
of the heavenly Jerusalem.[34]

Unceasing prayer gives us the strength we need to radiate joy amidst pain; to be gentle when others grate on our nerves; and to challenge, with a faith that moves mountains, anyone who foolishly assumes that life ends with death.

LET US PRAY

Lord, grant that my whole being may be an embodiment of your eternal, infinite love for souls. Since daily I may offend you, daily let me repent, saying, "I adore you and bless you because

by your holy cross you have redeemed the world." Let me be like a burning candle whose flame stays bright amidst the shadows of life that would obscure its light. May my prayers be like incense spreading its fragrance to every corner of the sanctuary, symbolizing the bond between earth and heaven, and strengthening the membership you have graciously granted me in your Mystical Body. Amen.

PART FOUR
SENT INTO THE WORLD

✦❧✦❧

✦❧✦❧

I. ATTRACTING OTHERS TO THE LORD

The gladness of the resurrection relieves the sadness we see in the world.

Try to find out what is pleasing to the Lord. Take no part in the unfruitful works of darkness, but instead expose them. For it is shameful even to mention what such people do secretly; but everything exposed by the light becomes visible, for everything that becomes visible is light. Therefore it says, "Sleeper awake! Rise from the dead, and Christ will shine on you" (Ephesians 5:10-14).

The light of Christ radiates with epiphanic splendor through humanity and history despite the shadows cast by the forces of hatred and hopelessness. Christ as fully human understands our condition with its limits and blessings. Christ as fully divine calls us by name and gives us a new identity, known only to him, so that we may be consecrated and sent forth to continue his mission in justice, peace, and mercy. Sin may abound, but it is no match for God's majestic plan for our salvation: "… God proves his love for us in that while we still were sinners Christ died for us. Much more surely then, now that we have been justified by his blood, we will be saved through him from the wrath of God. For while we were enemies, we were reconciled to God through the death of his Son, much more surely, having been reconciled, will we be saved by his life. But more than that, we even boast in God through our Lord Jesus Christ, through whom we have now received reconciliation" (Romans 5:8-11).

The fourteenth-century mystic Blessed Henry Suso (c. 1300-1365) understood what our response to this encounter with Christ ought to be. He says: "Perfection does not consist in experiencing consolation. It consists in surrendering one's will to God's will, whether this be burdensome or easy … In this context I would prefer aridity with this obedience to overflowing sweetness without it. This was shown us in the obedience of the eternal Son, which was carried out in arid bitterness. I am not saying this so that you offer yourself for this, as many of you do, but that you suffer patiently and do the best you can … The Lord, who is the object of your striving, has put you in this position with no help from you. He can certainly look after what is best for you in accordance with what praises him and brings you eternal happiness."[35]

LET US PRAY

Lord, every time your love draws to itself my heart's longing, I see more clearly what in my character has to change for me to be more like you. A flood of affection replaces my fears. New avenues of ministry open before me. From this point onward, I make good decisions and put them in motion because I know you are acting in me through the power of your Spirit. Please continue to give direction to my mind, endurance to my spirit, and determination to my will. Amen.

✦✦✦✦✦

2. WORSHIPPING IN SPIRIT AND TRUTH
The thirst for God compels us to search for truth and to worship God as God wills.

Jesus said to her, "Woman, believe me, the hour is coming when you will worship the Father neither on this mountain nor in Jerusalem. You worship what you do not know; we worship what we know, for salvation is from the Jews. But the hour is coming, and is now here, when the true worshipers will worship the Father in spirit and truth, for the Father seeks such as these to worship him. God is spirit, and those who worship him must worship him in spirit and truth (John 4:21-24).

The clamor of constant activity tempts us to live unreflectively. While we may make excuses to avoid the call to worship, we cannot resist it forever. We begin to see that daily tasks take on a deeper meaning when we practice the presence of God. A change of heart begins to happen. We no longer allow hectic agitation to separate us from the inspirations of the Holy Spirit. Time becomes not a collection of moments to be filled but a manifestation of that mysterious hour whose coming is not ours to control.

Jean Pierre de Caussade (1675-1751) reveals in *Abandonment to Divine Providence* the secret to living in this worshipful stance: "Once we can grasp that each moment contains some sign of the will of God, we shall find in it all we can possibly desire, for there is nothing more reasonable, more excellent, more holy than this will. Can any variations of time, place or circumstance add anything to its infinite value? If you are taught the secret of finding its presence in every moment of your lives, then you possess all that is most precious and supremely worthwhile. What is it that you want—those of you seeking perfection? Give your desires free reign, setting absolutely no limits, no boundaries to them. Listen to me: let your hearts demand the infinite, for I can tell you how to fill them. There is never one moment in which I cannot show you how to find whatever it is you can desire. The present moment is always overflowing with immeasurable riches, far more then you are able to hold."[36]

When we wait upon the guidance of God instead of pushing our own agenda, we are more likely to bear lasting fruit in our ministry. We redirect our energy away from mere activism and towards accomplishing what God asks of us in God's good time.

Any split in ministry between the contemplative and the active life, between prayer and participation in the working places where we serve, is an illusion. We must never separate Mary who rested at the feet of Jesus from Martha working busily in the kitchen (Luke 10:38-42). Both women in their own way are to bring the Messiah's message to a world waiting to hear the Good News.

LET US PRAY

Lord, let your Spirit, praying in me, refine my sensitivity to the Father's will. Both in the light of certitude and in the darkness of unknowing, increase my belief that the Holy Spirit, my Divine Guide, gives me the inspirations I need to incarnate your will and subdue my own. Let me pray with humility and temper the tendency to take charge. Make me aware that every good deed I do is but a response to the gifts I receive from you. Amen.

✦✦✦✦✦

3. DRAWING OTHERS TO THE WELLSPRING OF DIVINE LOVE
By dying to self we draw others to God.

Then he said to them all, "If any want to become my followers, let them deny themselves and take up their cross daily and follow me. For those who want to save their life will lose it, and those who lose their life for my sake will save it" (Luke 9:23-24).

The kenotic, self-emptying core of Christ's character explains why he did not cling to anything, not even to his equality with God. He chose instead the condition of a servant, modeling what he taught by washing the apostle's feet and warning us never to boast of our own importance.

Father Walter Ciszek, SJ (1904-1984) sought this posture of submission during his twenty-year imprisonment in Russia. He had no choice but to practice continual self-effacement, because he knew what it was like to be reduced to nothing. Only then could he become the priest our Lord intended him to be. He writes: "There was no one to turn to, no one to talk to, no one from whom I could seek advice or sympathetic understanding, no one to offer me any consolation … The other roommates from the camp who had been arrested with us must all have been in other cells. And so, as I had done in every other crisis, I turned to God in prayer. I sought his help, his sympathy, his consolation. Since I was suffering especially for his sake, since I was despised precisely because I was one of his priests, he could not fail to comfort me when he himself, in his human life, had fitted Isaiah's description of 'despised and the most abject of men.' He too had sought for someone to comfort him and found none. Surely he could sympathize with my plight; surely he would comfort and console me."[37]

At his lowest ebb, this holy priest showed everyone around him—friend and foe—what redemptive love really meant. Every time he was tempted to rely on himself instead of turning to the Lord, he felt the full force of spiritual desolation. That was when he knew he had to return as swiftly as possible to the practice of prayer. Upon his release from prison, this man of God became "another Christ" and a superb director of souls. A few words, finely chosen by Father Walter, relieved troubled hearts and strengthened one's relationship with God. Inspired by the psalmist, he must have prayed:

"My eyes are ever turned toward the Lord, for he will pluck my feet out of the net. Turn to me and be gracious to me, for I am lonely and afflicted. Relieve the troubles of my heart, and bring me out of my distress. Consider my affliction and my trouble and forgive all my sins" (Psalm 25:15-18).

LET US PRAY

Lord, my life is like a doomed land. Instead of lamenting my loss, teach me to enter into that stream of Divine Love flowing from the Trinity into the core of my being. Break through the dykes of my self-centeredness. Release the rushing waters of sanctity and service so that your people will be parched no more. Amen.

✦❖✦

4. BECOMING MESSENGERS OF THE MYSTERY
We need to hear and obey God's word before we can convey it to others.

But Moses said to the people, "Do not be afraid, stand firm, and see the deliverance that the Lord will accomplish for you today; for the Egyptians whom you shall see today you shall never see again. The Lord will fight for you, and you have only to keep still" (Exodus 14:13-14).

To serve the Lord as messengers of his mystery, we need to meditate on his words in silence and only then to speak. The Quaker spiritual writer Douglas V. Steere (1901-1995) says in this regard: "I believe that in the period that lies ahead, there is no deeper challenge in our personal, spiritual, and social witness all over the globe than this issue of learning to be present where we are in our personal relationships and making our witness and effort to rouse men and women to dare to be present to each other. The issue of peace and war, the issue of racial tensions, the issue of an educational breakthrough, the issue of our responsibility to contribute to the quickening of the relationships of the great world religions—all come down in the end to this daring to be present where we are."[38]

The lesson Steere wants us to learn is that God accepts our weary body as much as our listless spirit. When it seems as if fatigue has penetrated every fiber of our being, we may be humble enough to admit that God alone can give us the spiritual stamina we need to start again. When we derive our strength from the Lord, we may notice that ordinary tasks, which seem to lack meaning, become channels of divine illumination. Legend has it that when the Blessed Virgin Mary picked up a needle that had fallen to the floor in her modest abode in Nazareth, so lovingly did she do so that graces flowed from her being into every crevice of the cosmos. This story teaches us never to doubt the efficacy of the humblest tasks we perform, from making beds in the morning to covering those sleeping in them at night. We need not trouble ourselves about the degree of their importance in God's reign. What matters in fulfilling the call to discipleship is not outward success but inward fidelity.

LET US PRAY

Lord, whether I sail on rough or restful waters, remind me that you are the captain of my ship. Steer me toward calmer seas beyond the pressures of sheer busyness. The moment monotonous chores become acts of loving fidelity, I am on the path to living a life full of meaning. I can go forward without fear, abandoned to you and as active and contemplative as you allow me to be. Amen.

✦⊱✦⊰

5. MOVING FROM PRIDE TO HUMILITY

Every yielding to God's will increases our humility and readies us for service to God and neighbor.

Therefore, to keep me from being too elated, a thorn was given to me in the flesh, a messenger of Satan to torment me, to keep me from being too elated. Three times I appealed to the Lord about this, that it would leave me, but he said to me, "My grace is sufficient for you, for power is made perfect in weakness." So, I will boast all the more gladly of my weaknesses, so that the power of Christ may dwell in me. Therefore I am content with weaknesses, insults, hardships, persecutions, and calamities for the sake of Christ; for whenever I am weak, then I am strong (2 Corinthians 12:7-10).

The agony of our crucified savior was without consolation, yet his only desire was to fulfill the Father's will.
To follow him, we, too, must deny ourselves and take up
our crosses with love and total trust. Whatever poses a hin-
drance to this depth of discipleship must be purged if we
are to move from pride to humility, from the illusion of
power to the powerlessness of the cross.

In his inspiring treatise, *True Christianity*, Johann Arndt
(1555-1621) observes: "If you cannot bring to your beloved
God many and great offerings such as meditation, prayer,
and thanksgiving, bring to him what you have and can, and
with these, a good will and holy desires, and hope that you
might please him in your worship. To have such a holy desire, indeed, to wish to have one, is not a small gift or sacrifice. It, too, pleases God."[39]

Our fear of failure flees when we realize that God does
not demand more from us than his grace at work in us enables. Scripture confirms that "There is no fear in love, but
perfect love casts out fear" (1 John 4:18). Who knew this truth
better than the famed evangelist, Corrie Ten Boom (1892-
1983), who confesses in *The Hiding Place*: "... as the rest of the
world grew stranger, one thing became increasingly clear.
And that was the reason the two of us were here ... from
morning until lights-out ... our Bible was the center of an ev-
er-widening circle of help and hope ... The blacker the night
around us grew, the brighter and truer and more beautiful
burned the word of God. 'Who shall separate us from the
love of Christ? Shall tribulation, or distress, or persecution,
or famine, or nakedness, or peril, or sword? ... Nay, in all
these things we are more than conquerors through him that
loved us.' ... More than conquerors ... It was not a wish. It
was a fact ... the life we lived with God, grew daily better,
truth upon truth, glory upon glory."[40]

Throughout their time of imprisonment by the Nazi occupiers of their country, Corrie and her saintly sister Betsie continued to offer the other women in the camps every opportunity to survive with dignity. To bear lasting fruit, as the Lord commands, can never happen in a world where injustice, lack of peace, and a dearth of compassion prevail. Both sisters did all they could under conditions of severe deprivation to draw forth everyone's potential for doing what was right and good, whether the soup was cold and tasteless or the fleas invasive of every bunk in the barracks. Even when they were tempted to see only the negative side of their situation, they chose to focus on the smallest positive signs of God's care. After all, the fleas were the reason the guards left them alone. They could then read their Bible aloud to a rapt yet ravished group of desperate women.

LET US PRAY

Thank you, Lord, for being the source of my peace in times of profound distress. Help me to forego feelings of unforgiveness by showing kindness to friend and foe. Let me reclaim my freedom to be of service to all. Let me see that my growth in the spiritual life does not depend on what I do but on what you do in and through me. Whether I fail or succeed, I pray that my primary desire will always be to remain pleasing in your sight. Amen.

✦⊰⊱✦

6. BECOMING LIKE LITTLE CHILDREN

God wants us to become like little children who welcome his gifts with open arms.

People were bringing even infants to him that he might touch them; and when the disciples saw it, they sternly ordered them not to do it. But Jesus called for them and said, "Let the little children come to me,

*and do not stop them; for it is to such as these that the kingdom of God
belongs. Truly I tell you, whoever does not receive the kingdom of God
as a little child will never enter it" (Luke 18:15-17).*

There are times when life takes such a nasty turn that it
wounds us to the core, flattens our hopes for the future,
and scares us into inactivity. Life slips out of our control and
carries us along like falling leaves drifting aimlessly across
windy streets. The daily grind seems devoid of direction
with little or no relief in sight. Such is the downward spin
into feelings of our having been abandoned by God.

Instead of thinking we can make sense out of nonsense
by virtue of our own cleverness, we need to take another
turn. There is nothing we can do for the moment but let
ourselves be cradled like little children in the Lord's arms.
Only his love is strong enough to dig into the dank well of
discouragement and rid us of its debris.

The opposite option of appreciative abandonment to
the Mystery sets us on a new course. The danger of the crisis
that engulfed us gives way to the opportunity to change our
whole outlook on life. We enter into a kind of second inno-
cence, aware of sin but never doubting the power of salvific
love and forgiveness.

A spokeswoman for the little way of spiritual childhood
is St. Thérèse of Lisieux (1873-1897). In her *Story of a Soul*, she
offers us this memorable description of letting go of self-de-
ceptive illusions and accepting fully who we are: "I am only
a child, powerless and weak, and yet it is my weakness that
gives me the boldness of offering myself as *Victim of Your
Love, O Jesus!* In times past, victims, pure and spotless, were
the only ones accepted by the Strong and Powerful God. To
satisfy Divine *Justice,* perfect victims were necessary, but the
law of Love has succeeded to the law of fear, and *Love* has

chosen me as a holocaust, me, a weak and imperfect creature. Is not this choice worthy of *Love*? Yes, in order that
Love be fully satisfied, it is necessary that it lower Itself to
nothingness and transform this nothingness into *fire*."[41]

The ways of the Lord may defy understanding, but that
is all the more reason for us to behave with unfaltering trust.
Counsels like the following from the Book of Proverbs fos-
ter the power of appreciation and teach us how to put it
into practice: "Trust in the Lord with all your heart, and do
not rely on your own insight. In all your ways acknowledge
him, and he will make straight your paths. Do not be wise
in your own eyes; fear the Lord, and turn away from evil. It
will be a healing for your flesh and a refreshment for your
body" (Proverbs 3:5-8).

LET US PRAY

*Lord, carry me beyond childish fears to childlike trust in you.
A situation that seems hopeless starts to improve the minute I
detect in this obstacle a formation opportunity. Your promise to be
with me always gives me the courage to move from lamenting my
fate to welcoming the challenges life poses. You may write straight
with crooked lines, but it is a delight to decipher your words in the
divinely inspired dictionary of faith, hope, and love. Amen.*

✛➳❁✛➳

7. Growing in Spiritual Friendship
*Of more worth than fame or worldly gain is the gift of a faithful
friend.*

*Faithful friends are a sturdy shelter: whoever finds one has found a
treasure. Faithful friends are beyond price; no amount can balance
their worth. Faithful friends are life-saving medicine; and those*

who fear the Lord direct their friendship aright, for as they are, so are their neighbors also (Sirach 6:14-17).

Spiritual friendship is a gift beyond price; it cannot be forced; it comes to us as an unexpected blessing. Friends encourage us to fulfill our calling in Christ and help us to overcome countless problems. Mere acquaintances tend to remain at a distance from one another. Without a bonding of two hearts in the Lord, we risk becoming preoccupied with individual achievements. We fall into the trap of thinking we can manage life on our own.

St. Francis de Sales (1567-1622) shares his experience of being friends in the Lord, saying, "If your mutual and reciprocal exchanges concern charity, devotion, and Christian perfection, O God, how precious this friendship will be! It will be excellent because it comes from God, excellent because it leads to God, excellent because its bond will endure eternally in God. How good it is to love here on earth as they love in heaven and to learn to cherish one another in this world as we shall do eternally in the next!"[42]

When we are with a true friend, the time we spend together passes in a flash. It feels as if we could talk forever. Here is a person with whom we can engage in trusting exchanges that are always life-giving. We feel comfortable enough with our friend to celebrate our kinships as well as our differences. If our friendship is a healthy one, both of us gain the strength to be who we truly are. We know that our life is precious in our friend's eyes. His or her respect fills us with gratitude and readies us to respond as the unique persons we are to our commonality in the Lord.

We know that we are destined, despite our diversity, to dwell in time and eternity in the homeland prepared for us by our Divine Friend in whose house there are many dwelling places. Who else but a friend would go before us to prepare a place for us, since where Our Lord is there also shall we be (John 14:3).

LET US PRAY

Lord, let my friendship with you be the basis of every faithful sharing I enjoy with my brothers and sisters. May others know, through the light in my eyes and the smile on my lips, how much I love them as reflections of you. In life and death bind us to the family of the Trinity with cords of communion nothing can break. Feed us, Lord, with the bread of heaven so that I and my friends may know from experience the lasting fruits of your compassionate care and concern. Let the Christ in me meet and greet the Christ in them. Amen.

EPILOGUE

Spiritual hunger seems to reach epidemic proportions when, despite the promises for fulfillment promulgated by purveyors of power, pleasure, or possession, nothing fills that hole in our heart that belongs only to God. No amount of attempted mastery of natural or supernatural forces can quell the gnawing experience of our being dependent on a mystery beyond our control.

A retreat from the pain of the present moment to the mythical safety of a nostalgic past does not diminish our anxiety. While we need to respect the wisdom of what was, we have no choice but to accept with courage what is and will be. The future is in God's hands, not ours. The journey of faith on which we have embarked in response to God's grace involves risk and conflict, but waters unstirred grow stagnant. We need to reflect on what these changes mean.

Consider the plight of parents sending their children off to school. They worry less about how to fill the empty nest and more about how well these young adults will handle their new-found freedom. Will they remember the rules of moral conduct they were taught? Are the classes and churches they attend, are the safety nets provided by their schools, enough to protect them from irresponsible behavior and outbreaks of violence?

Neither over- nor under-protection can prevent a calamity from occurring. Parents need to pray that their children's decisions will be guided by God — and that their children place others' needs before their own. Sensitivity and responsibility are dispositions of the Christian heart that nourish our spiritual hunger and help us to reform the selfish remnants that may still cling like barnacles to our personhood.

Under the guise of helping others, we may place our own "do-gooding" image first. The solution to selfishness is not found with the snap of a finger. This gift of God may only be granted to us after many dark nights. As we begin to change from within, we may notice that others around us change too.

To monitor the depth or shallowness of our spirituality, we might ask: Why do we get upset when others do not act according to the list of "shoulds" we are eager to supply? Are our concerns really compassionate or are they rooted in seductive ploys to have the last word? Are we willing to face the consequences of eroded relationships and try to better them by forgiveness? Do we prefer to talk through the predicaments in which we find ourselves rather than becoming defensive and refusing to listen to what others have to say? Most of all, do we ask God to detach us from the collection of self-preoccupations that continue to plague our relations with family members and friends?

Such prayerful reflection engaged in with like-minded others prevents us from being swayed by superficial solutions to every dilemma. When an obstacle presents itself, we need to unpack the formation opportunity embedded in it. No plant can grow strong unless it resists being choked by weeds. Spiritual hunger may be God's way of freeing us from the clutches of complacency and readying us to receive the grace of ongoing conversion.

Where our treasure is, Scripture tells us, there our heart is to be found. Every nugget of wisdom recorded in this book, be it from Scripture or the masters, serves to touch and transform us from within and without. When and if we suffer, we know it is for the sake of growing in virtue. We learn in a culture suffocated by lies that only the truth can set us free. We admire the courage of people willing to be martyred for their faith and shake our heads in sadness that the word *love*, when it's not exemplified in deeds, is meaningless.

My hope is that this book will be read and reread and that its teachers will become our friends. We need these lasting treasures, beginning with the italicized words of Father Adrian van Kaam, to strengthen our convictions and remind us of what is perennially true.[43] Here are the rock solid foundations on which our house of faith can and should be built. Then we can live with the assurance that the treasures unearthed here will last us through time and onward to eternity.

In the meantime we can review and reflect upon the last spiritual counsels Father Adrian left us. In summary, they are:

1. Being Called Friends. The gift of friendship mirrors God's befriending of us.

2. Healed by Christ's wounds. The delectable pain of the wound of love is a comfort to my soul.

3. Advancing in Wisdom. To follow the way of wisdom is to live in cordial intimacy with the Trinity.

4. Experiencing Steadfast Love. Because God loves us as a mother loves her child, God wants us to care for one another.

5. Becoming More Faithful. Fidelity is the endless symphony that binds our wayward being to the Trinity.

6. Changing Our Heart. God hides in the hermitage of our heart.

7. Finding True Happiness. True happiness resides in our total abandonment to the Beloved.

✦✦✦✦✦

1.   **Freedom from Self-Seeking**. Every epiphany of the mystery is an invitation to be free from selfish acquisitions.

2.   **Practicing the Presence of God**. The hunger in our heart can never be satisfied until we experience lasting union with God.

3.   **Growing in Compassion**. In the mirror of our compassion others see the face of Christ.

4.   **Becoming "Little Words" in the Eternal Word**. The Word of God is alive in every longing heart.

5.   **Living in Forgiveness**. Forgiveness only makes sense when we stand with open arms at the foot of the cross.

6.   **Proclaiming God's Power in Powerlessness**. Powerlessness readies us to accept the power that flows forth from the cross.

7. Remaining Resilient in the Face of Adversity. Adversity is the soil in which joyful resilience abounds.

✦✦✦✦✦

1.   **Living in Humility**. Seeing our limits as blessings opens our hearts to the grace of humility.

2. **Lifted to New Levels of Spiritual Awakening**. Grace lifts us to levels of spiritual awakening beyond imagining.

3. **Denying Ourselves to Follow Jesus**. The Holy Spirit implants in our soul the "yes" of the Son to the will of the Father.

4. **Moving from Desolation to Consolation**. The farther away God seems, the nearer God is to hearts who seek him without ceasing.

5. **Enjoying the Fruits of Discipleship**. The more we efface ourselves, the more room there is for the light of the Lord to shine through us.

6. **Being Attuned to the Pace of God's Grace**. The secret of staying with grace is to remember that love unending has already given us the grace to do so.

7. **Becoming Living Prayer**. Living prayer is the practice of ceaseless communion with God who dwells within us.

✦⊱⊰✦

1. **Attracting Others to the** Lord. The gladness of the resurrection relieves the sadness we see in the world.

2. **Worshipping in Spirit and T**ruth. The thirst for God compels us to search for truth and to worship God as God wills.

3. **Drawing Others to the Wellspring of Divine** Love. By dying to self we draw others to God.

4. **Becoming Messengers of the Mys**tery. We need to hear and obey God's word before we can convey it to others.

5. **Moving from Pride to Humi**lity. Every yielding to God's will increases our humility and readies us for service to God

and neighbor.

6. **Becoming Like Little Children**. God wants us to become like little children who welcome His gifts with open arms.

7. **Growing in Spiritual Friendship**. Of more worth than fame or worldly gain is the gift of a faithful friend.

MEET THE MASTERS

AELRED OF RIEVAULX, ST. (1109-1167). Inspired by the reforming spirit of St. Bernard of Clairvaux (1090-1153), Aelred entered the Rievaulx Abbey in England in 1134. In the Benedictine rule he found the key to monastic life: contemplation as the ground of Christian charity, with spiritual friendship as its finest fruit. Because of his firm yet gentle leadership, Abbot Aelred attracted over six hundred monks to his monastery.

ARNDT, JOHANN (1555-1621). Of great inspiration to this Lutheran theologian were *The Imitation of Christ* by Thomas à Kempis (1380-1471) and the *Sermons* of John Tauler (c. 1300-1361). He wrote four books on true Christianity, placing great emphasis on conversion and holy living. Arndt taught and lived this truth: Christian fellowship with God and others offers us a foretaste of eternity.

AUGUSTINE OF HIPPO, ST. (354-430). One of the most influential and prolific of the Fathers and Doctors of Western Christendom, this famous convert to Christianity left a lasting legacy to the Church in masterpieces like *The Confessions*, *The City of God*, and *On the Trinity*. Ordained a priest in 391, he then became Bishop of Hippo in North Africa in 395, an office he held for thirty-five years. During this time he founded a religious community; wrote the Augustinian rule, with its emphasis on charity as the goal of the Christian life; and defended, against a floodtide of heresy, the foundational teachings he derived from the two wings of truth: reason and faith.

BENEDICT OF NURSIA, ST. (480-543). The Father of Western monasticism lived at a time when civilization was on the threshold of decline and devastation, but this dark age could not dim the radiance of this future saint, miracle-worker, and author of a rule of life that continues to flourish, thanks to its perennial balance of prayer and work, contemplation and charitable action. Benedict taught his monks to follow the fourfold path of *lectio divina* (sacred reading), *meditatio* (meditative reflection), *oratio* (prayer), and *contemplatio* (contemplation). The perennial practice of such virtues as obedience, humility, compunction of heart, and ongoing conversion led the community to moderation in all things and respect for each person's calling in Christ.

BONAVENTURE, ST. (1221-1274). This saint, spiritual master, and Doctor of the Church, was a loyal and loving follower of St. Francis of Assisi (1182-1226) and his principal biographer. Bonaventure synthesized the meaning of Christian mysticism in his masterpiece, *The Soul's Journey into God*, in which he traces six degrees of ascent to mystical union with the Blessed Trinity. In his life and work, he reveals an exemplary integration of the love of learning and the desire for God.

BONHOEFFER, DIETRICH (1906-1945). Following his call to true discipleship, this brilliant Lutheran pastor was a teacher and professor of theology in Spain, America, and England, as well as in his home country of Germany. Soon after the rise of Nazism, he became an out-

spoken critic of the regime and an active member of the resistance movement. He was arrested and imprisoned by the
Gestapo and executed two years later. He wrote, in addition
to his letters and papers from prison, his Christian classic,
The Cost of Discipleship, in which he challenges every reader
to reflect on what it means to be a messenger of Christ in a
secular world.

CARRETTO, CARLO (1910-1988) was deeply
committed to his vocation with the Fraternity of the Little
Brothers of Jesus and their worldwide mission to integrate
the desert and the city. Carretto had received his religious
education at a Salesian Oratory, which emphasized Catholic action. When Carretto began his novitiate with the Little
Brothers on December 8, 1954, he saw it as the culmination
of ten years of searching for and finding God in silence,
prayer, and work. These are the central themes in many of
his books. When he died on October 4, 1988, on the feast day
of St. Francis of Assisi, hundreds of people from Italy and
abroad came to pay tribute to the selfless monk, whose *alter
christus* way of life had called them to conversion.

CATHERINE OF SIENA, ST. (1347-1380).
Destined to become the patron saint of Italy, this future
Doctor of the Church had at the age of six a vision of Christ
the King. This mystical encounter sealed her vocation to
wed only her heavenly spouse. Catherine grew from being
an unschooled and illiterate laywoman to being a spiritual guide and counselor to popes as well as common folks.
Having been taught to read through the intervention of the
Holy Spirit, she helped to resolve the Great Schism in Avignon that tore at the fabric of the papacy. Her masterpiece,
The Dialogue, delves into God's truth and the humility of
mind that is the seedbed of pure faith.

CISZEK, FATHER WALTER J. (1904-1984).

This Jesuit priest, author of two contemporary classics, *With God in Russia* and *He Leadeth Me*, teaches by example what it means to live in abandonment to Divine Providence. He hoped, after ordination, to be missioned to the Soviet Union. Thus, in 1938, he was assigned to eastern Poland, where he joined the Polish refugees fleeing the invasion of Red Army troops. Two years later it felt to him as if his mission had come to an end when he was arrested by the Soviet Secret Police and sentenced to fifteen years of hard labor, worsened by solitary confinement for five years in the infamous Lubianka Prison in Moscow. Harassment by the KGB, who wrested from him a false confession, became for him the breakthrough to true humility and the meaning of heroic virtue in imitation of Christ. Father Walter was released in 1963 as part of a prisoner exchange and spent the remaining twenty years of his life serving others as a spiritual guide and a saintly witness to the heroic virtues and merits gained through the trial of faith.

CLARE OF ASSISI, ST. (1193-1254).

The beloved daughter of a noble Italian family, Clare refused two offers of marriage, but she did not make up her mind to leave the world until she came under the influence of the Poor Man of God, St. Francis of Assisi. At the age of eighteen, Clare left home secretly under his direction and knew from the first moment she heard him preach that she had found her vocation. From then on, she never wavered in her determination to live for Lady Poverty. Clare became the Abbess of the Poor Clares and guided her community with discretion for forty years. During that time, other Claretian convents were established throughout Europe, all inspired by her rule of life, her love of prayer, and her service of the materially and spiritually poor.

DAY, DOROTHY (1897-1980). The future co-founder with Peter Maurin (1877-1949) of the Catholic Worker Movement converted to Catholicism after the birth of her daughter. She wished to dedicate her life to service of the poor by means of living the corporal works of mercy: to feed the hungry, clothe the naked, and shelter the homeless. Her ideals of social action were fulfilled in her commitment to human rights and the cause of non-violence. Her autobiography, *The Long Loneliness*, became a best seller due to its unforgettable rendition of her own and every soul's deep yearning toward God. For Day, this longing could only be satisfied by her lifelong devotion to the Eucharist, coupled with her dedication to serve with tireless devotion every member of the mystical body of Christ.

DE CAUSSADE, JEAN-PIERRE (1675-1781). This renowned confessor and spiritual director was a member of the Society of Jesus. His gifts for teaching and preaching inspired especially the religious congregations he served. His many conferences to the nuns of the Order of the Visitation in Nancy, France, were preserved by them. The conferences remained unpublished until 1861, when they found their way into print under the title of *Abandonment to Divine Providence*, which became from its first printing onward a spiritual classic. De Caussade points to the action of the Divine Will in everyday life. For him trusting surrender to God is the essence of spirituality as well as the supreme duty of our existence. Standing on this foundation enables us to see all that happens to us, be it joyful or painful, as an expression of God's love, leading us to a life as peaceful as it is productive.

FRANCIS DE SALES, ST. (1567-1622). True to the obedience characteristic of the discipleship he preached, Francis followed, at first, his family's wishes that he study to be a lawyer, but upon attaining his degree he listened to the voice of God within his heart and pursued the priesthood rather than a lucrative career. His ministry centered on Catholic life in the region of Lake Geneva, where he excelled in both civil and canon law in a predominantly Calvinist area of France. Within three years he became the bishop there and won over the district with his gentle heart and sense of self-sacrifice, virtues he strove to bestow on the faithful he served. Among them was the saintly widow, Jane Frances de Chantel, who under his direction would eventually become the founder of a new religious community for women: Visitation of Holy Mary. In his masterpiece, *Introduction to the Devout Life* (1608), Francis appealed to his readers to develop their spirituality not apart from, but in the midst of, their ordinary circumstances, and to see them as occasions of grace.

ECKHART, MEISTER (1260-1329). A Dominican friar, renowned for his theological brilliance, Eckhart earned the title of "Meister." He complemented his scholarly teaching with instructions to the faithful. In his famous treatise "On Detachment," he defined his central concepts concerning the relationship between the human and the divine. Eckhart held that other-centered love and service demands self-emptying and detachment, lest illusory attachments impede progress to union and the grace of allowing God's word to be born anew in our soul. While some propositions in his writing came under ecclesiastical scrutiny in his time, all such bans were eventually lifted by the Church.

ELIZABETH OF THE TRINITY, ST. (1880-1906).

This French Carmelite was a gifted pianist, a vivacious child, and, from the time of her First Communion on April 19, 1891, a lover of God to whose glory she pledged the rest of her life. So attracted was Elizabeth to interior prayer that she begged to be admitted to Carmel, but, sadly for her, she had to finish her education before entering the Carmel of Dijon at the age of twenty-one. Once there, she devoted herself to following her rule of silence, spiritual reading of Scripture and the masters, and obedience to her superiors. She had a deep devotion to the Blessed Trinity and longed to bury herself in this abyss of Pure Love. Her life ended with the excruciating suffering associated with Addison's disease. Throughout this ordeal, she never lost the joy of feeling the presence of God, writing shortly before her death that her mission in heaven would be to encourage souls to enter into their inmost self and to allow God to transform their humanity into an incarnation of his divinity.

GREGORY THE GREAT, ST. (540-604).

Amid the ruins of the crumbling Roman Empire, this saint interrupted a brilliant public career, turned his palatial residence into a Benedictine monastery, and dedicated his entire diplomatic and priestly life to God. Until 584 he was Papal Nuncio to Constantinople; he would have preferred to serve the Church in relative obscurity but in 590 he was elected Pope, calling himself a "servant of God's servants." In trying to uphold the administrative, pastoral, social, ecclesial, and moral claims of an ideal Christian society, Pope Gregory pursued at all times the integration of contemplation and action. In addition to codifying the seven capital sins and reforming liturgical ritual and music, notably with Gregorian chant, he accepted the burden and blessing of caring with tireless devotion, despite his own failing health, for the spiritual and material welfare of the people of God.

HADEWIJCH (D. 1282). A Flemish beguine, a member of the most notable women's movement of her day, Hadewijch desired to emulate the hidden life of Jesus of Nazareth. However, in the providence of God, this visionary woman from Antwerp became known for the dual gifts of mystical union and literary genius. Committed to living her discipleship in the "cloister of the world," she directed her words of wisdom and her works of charity to the younger members of her community. She taught them by example that love for the humanity and divinity of God's only begotten Son would enable them to know the Lord and to serve others as selflessly as he did.

JOHN OF THE CROSS, ST. (1542-1591). The poverty of this future saint's childhood in the town of Medina del Campo, Spain, taught him the meaning of compassion for humanity and inspired his entrance in 1564 to the Carmelite community. He displayed such brilliance that he was sent after his novitiate to study at the University of Salamanca, where he wrote his thesis on the theme of fidelity to the doctrine of the Church. After his ordination in 1567, it became clear to him that God had other plans for his life—not to follow a university career but to be a reformer, along with St. Teresa of Avila, of the Carmelite Order itself. The poverty he loved would be symbolized in the Discalced charism of the Order in accordance with the way of life prescribed by their twelfth century founder, St. Albert of Jerusalem. John would go on to write exquisite poetry, singing of the exchanges of love between the soul and God. His commentary on his own poetry, much of it composed during a nine-month imprisonment by his original order, led to its companion texts—masterpieces of ascetical-mystical theology, including *The Ascent of Mount Carmel*, *The Dark Night*, *The Spiritual Canticle*, and *The Living Flame of Love*. This Doctor of the Church died as he had lived, on December 14, 1591, in peace and poverty of soul, knowing that he had been permitted by grace to drink from the cup of Christ's own suffering and thereby, in his words, to have penetrated "deep into the thicket of the delectable wisdom of God."

JULIAN OF NORWICH (1342-1373). This fourteenth-century English mystic and solitary anchoress lived in a cell attached to the Church of St. Julian in Norwich, England. When she was thirty years old and in the throes of a near-fatal illness, she experienced a series of sixteen revelations about Jesus and Mary and the Tempter, who seeks to devour any semblance of saintliness. For the rest of her life, she pondered the meaning of these showings and the challenge catastrophic circumstances like the Black Plague posed to one's faith. Julian gained the reputation of being one of the holiest and wisest of the English spiritual writers, admired by scholars as well as the common folk with whom she identified. All who read her work were struck by her hopeful, appreciative spirit, and her repeated claim that "all shall be well and all manner of things shall be well." For Julian the presence of God was everywhere. A favorite symbol of hers was the hazelnut—such a small bit of creation, but the God who made it loves and preserves it as he does all of us. Christ died on the cross to save us; he cares for us as does a mother for her child. That is why Julian celebrates the maternal tenderness of Christ's humanity alongside the saving grace of his divinity, maintaining her conviction that love, not sin, is the ultimate meaning of our existence.

KELLY, THOMAS R. (1893-1941). A devout Quaker and author of the contemporary classic *A Testament of Devotion*, Kelly had a degree in theology from Harvard University and taught philosophy at Haverford College, among other institutes of higher learning. What drew Kelly beyond the pursuit of a career in academic life was his love for interior prayer. He discovered from his reading and his personal experience that within each of us is a Light that, if attended to, yields the grace of inner worship and a sense of the presence of God wherever we are. When Christ calls, our response must be one of holy obedience and unreserved surrender. Belonging to the blessed community of lovers and followers of Christ teaches us the efficacy of holy living and holy dying. For Kelly, our daily life ought to be an experience of the Eternal penetrating time and of the Sacred embodying itself in social action.

KIERKEGAARD, SØREN (1813-1855). Following an unhappy love affair and controversial, often condemnatory encounters with his peers, this famous philosopher from Copenhagen turned his attention to what living the Gospel demands of anyone who embraces the faith. Soon after he completed his study of theology, Kierkegaard considered taking orders in the Lutheran Church, but the philosophical work he had begun became his primary occupation. He is famous as well for his exemplary spiritual meditations, notably his preparation for the office of Confession, titled *Purity of Heart Is to Will One Thing*. Kierkegaard believed that one who wills the Good must be willing to do or suffer all for God and never stoop to being double-minded and entrapped in the entanglements of self-interest. He shunned the crowd mentality and a superficial living of "Christendom" and counseled his readers to strive over a lifetime to will "the one thing needful"—what God wills that we may reach the full promise of Christian perfection.

LAW, WILLIAM (1686-1761). Numbered among the greatest of the post-Reformation English mystics, an ordained priest in the Anglican Church, Law felt that his "serious call to a devout and holy life" was incompatible with the tenets of the Age of Reason, as well as with the loyalty oaths to the crown, which priests and professors were required to take. Instead he became the leader of a small spiritual community, including among his disciples John and Charles Wesley. For him devotion must entail not an occasional practice but the whole of one's human and spiritual life. One must intend to please God in all that one does. Merciful as the Lord is, our love for him should guide our intention to avoid sin and turn our lives to the service of God and neighbor. Unless our life matches our prayers, Law cautioned, we are liable to become only "lip laborers." True devotion removes the turmoil of an uncontrolled heart and, in his words, draws us to "imitate the higher perfections of the angels."

LAWRENCE OF THE RESURRECTION, BROTHER (1611-1691). Born in France, Nicholas Herman served in the army and worked as a household employee before deciding to enter the Discalced Carmelite order. Though he assumed a new name, Brother Lawrence, he remained a humble worker, finding his vocation among the pots and pans he cleaned in the kitchen and the shoes he mended as the community cobbler. For forty years he felt

drawn to unceasing prayer, which meant for him to practice the presence of God. A memoir published in his name
became a Christian classic. He tells how his life, simple as
it was, drew him to the heart of God. The ordinary chores
we undertake mark the place where God's grace can operate freely, thanks to the diligent practice of our doing everything to please the Lord. Brother Lawrence repeated as
often as he could, in his letters and conversations, that we
ought to live in the present moment and count on God to
give us what we need when we need it. In due course, he
said, prayer will become as natural to us as breath. Recog-
nized as a spiritual guide by religious and laity alike, Brother Lawrence lived an exemplary life and died a holy death
at the age of eighty.

NOUWEN, HENRI (1932-1996). Priest, spiritual
guide, author, and counselor, Nouwen insisted that the call
of Jesus is a call to conversion of heart and inner healing,
addressed not merely to saints but to people in everyday
life. He saw in the brokenness of humanity the wounded
and glorified body of Jesus. No matter how lost one felt,
he counseled, the way to one's true home could be found
through God's unlimited and unconditional love. Originally
from the Netherlands, Nouwen spent most of his life in the
United States, teaching at places like the Divinity Schools of
Harvard and Yale, and taking time off to live in a Trappist
abbey as well as among the poor in Latin America. He found
his final home in the L'Arche community called Daybreak
in Toronto, in a house devoted to the care of handicapped
people. At L'Arche, Nouwen felt the full impact of what it
meant to be a "wounded healer" for whom life itself becomes a preparation for death. He died of a heart attack in
his native Holland at the age of sixty-four.

PSEUDO-DIONYSIUS (C. 500). This enigmatic yet profoundly influential spiritual figure, possibly a Syrian monk of the sixth century, wrote under the pseudonym of Dionysius the Areopagite. His writings reveal a distinct preference for the *via negativa*, which stresses the utter inability of the human mind to penetrate the mystery of God. In his seminal book, *The Mystical Theology*, he introduces the threefold path of purgation, illumination, and union. These stages demarcate movements in the human soul responsive to divine transformation. Dionysius believed that God is above all names. He is a Being beyond being itself, residing in the dark reality of the super-essential nature of the Godhead that always and forever defies definition. Dionysius stresses the impotence of every human attempt to penetrate the veil that stands between God and us. God draws us through purification to deification. We must bow in humility before his allness and acknowledge our nothingness.

STEERE, DOUGLAS V. (1900-1995). A professor emeritus at Haverford College, an eminent spiritual guide and author, translator of works by Søren Kierkegaard, and editor of selected writings by Baron Friedrich von Hügel, Steere built bridges between Protestantism and Catholicism as well as between Christians and non-Christians. In his devotional books, many inspired by the Quaker tradition, he said that the ground of good conversation, and, by extension, the wellspring of prayer and worship, is listening in silence. The Friends trust that the Holy Spirit will evoke what they call "concerns." Virtues like vulnerability, acceptance, expectancy, and constancy are characteristic of good listeners. Steere also expressed the conviction that within every genuine conversation the Eternal Listener, the Living God, is present, clarifying confusion and enabling illuminating disclosures to emerge. For Steere, adoration stirs a desire in the soul to penetrate further into the abyss of being that puts us at the disposal of God and renews our commitment to the love and charitable works God requires of every true believer.

STEIN, EDITH, ST. TERESA BENEDICTA OF THE CROSS (1891-1942).

Jewish by birth and Catholic by faith, Edith was born in Breslau, Germany, on Yom Kippur, the Day of Atonement. Gifted with a philosophical mind and a writer's heart, she became at the University of Freiburg an assistant to Professor Edmund Husserl, the founder of the phenomenological movement. In 1922, when Edith was studying for her doctorate, she found the truth for which she had been searching in the teachings of Jesus Christ, and this encounter changed her life forever. Though her mother could not support her decision, Edith entered the Church. For the next ten years she continued to teach and write, achieving such a high degree of excellence that she was offered a professorship at the University of Münster. The following year the Nazis came to power. Many of her scholarly endeavors had to be curtailed, but this no longer disturbed her because she had set her heart on entering Carmel. Edith knew that nothing could protect her from the Nazi's hatred of the Jews, certainly not a convent grille. She tells us in her journals and letters that she prayed that God would accept her life and her death in expiation for people's disbelief, for the salvation of Germany, and for world peace. A mere eight years after her profession in 1935, her life would achieve its goal of self-surrender and the cross. When the Gestapo started persecuting religious orders in Cologne, Edith transferred to the Carmel in Echt, Holland. It was to no avail. In retaliation for a letter read by the Dutch bishops protesting the deportation of Jews, the Nazis rounded up Catholics of Jewish origin and sent them in July of 1942 to the concentration camp. Edith and Rosa Stein were among them. Her words to her sister were, "Come, Rosa, let us go for our people." The death of this prophetic witness to the sacredness of life occurred in Auschwitz on August 9, 1942.

SUSO, HENRY (1291-1366). Having grown up near Lake Constance on the border between Germany and Switzerland, Suso entered the Dominican friary at an early age. While in the monastery, he underwent a conversion experience and became a devoted follower of his fellow Dominican Meister Eckhart, whose cause he defended. He had to learn over the course of time that the road to the inner life was not paved by harsh physical chastisement, scrupulosity, or morbid asceticism, but by the practice of knowing and loving God in the suffering humanity of Jesus Christ, his only begotten Son. Destined to become one of the chief representatives of German mysticism, Suso shared with laity and religious his gifts for preaching and spiritual direction. In his richly lyrical and poetic writings, he fuses theological reflection and its application to everyday faith formation. His devotion to the divine name of Jesus and his disposition of perfect detachment so as "to receive everything from God" are key themes of his spirituality. Suso spent the last years of his life as an itinerant preacher and spiritual director of mainly the Dominican nuns and the Friends of God in Switzerland. He endured physical hardship and persecution by people who questioned his mission, but from start to finish he remained espoused to Lady Wisdom, in whose light all his longings found fulfillment.

TAULER, JOHN (1300-1361). This mystic and

spiritual master was above all a gifted preacher whose sermons educated and uplifted the soul. Tauler entered the Dominican Order in 1315, received a classical education, and spent his entire life preaching in towns and villages along the Rhine. He lived during a time of great turmoil in the Church. The pope was in exile in Avignon, famine and plague ravished the Continent, and new lay movements like the Beguines, the Brethren of the Free Spirit, and the Friends of God were on the rise. He favored the mystical life taught by Meister Eckhart with its stress on the indwelling Trinity and imageless contemplation, but he also preached about the beauty of the active life with devotion to Christ's poverty as an antidote to vanity and worldliness. Complementing Eckhart's teaching on the interior life, Tauler promoted a balanced appreciation of prayer in practice, of the right blend of activity and abandonment, revealing the affective and practical sides of mystical theology. He held that before ascending to God one must descend in humility to the foot of the cross, imitating Christ's self-emptying and abandonment to the will of the Father. Over eighty of his sermons remain in print and continue to inspire laity, clergy, and religious.

TEN BOOM, CORRIE (1892-1983).

From the safety net of their watchmaking shop, the Ten Boom family committed themselves to doing all they could to resist the Nazi invasion of their country and the persecution of its Jewish citizens. Corrie helped the family to hide a number of Jews and underground workers whose lives were at risk. Eventually their hiding place was discovered and Corrie and her sister Betsie were sent to the concentration camp at Ravensbruck. Humiliated, starving, and at the precipice of death (which soon claimed Betsie), the sisters ministered to the inmates by offering them from their cherished Bible access to God's loving and saving word. Corrie survived to tell the story of how faith ultimately triumphs over the most dehumanizing torture and tribulation. She became an evangelist from whose heart poured the inspiring message that God's love overcomes hate and heals and restores our souls. Her Christian classic, *The Hiding Place*, sheds light on one of the darkest moments of history and offers a strong reminder of the need for valor, determination, and heroic virtue in the face of any force that threatens our faith.

TERESA OF AVILA, ST. (1515-1582). Though this valiant woman struggled throughout her youth and early adulthood to find her true vocation, she knew already early in life that it was sheer foolishness to resist God's call. He revealed himself to her, after she entered the Monastery of the Incarnation in her home town of Avila, by making her feel uncomfortable with the mitigated style of life led by the nuns. She longed for the rigor of the original Carmelite rule, but it took some time before she saw in these inspirations a call for reform. Physical set-backs were familiar to her because she had a weak constitution, but no amount of trouble or misunderstanding could weaken her faith. Soon after reading the *Confessions of St Augustine*, she realized the need for ongoing conversion, a gift she received in 1554 while meditating before a statue depicting the scourging of Jesus at the pillar. Two years later, her spiritual espousal to Christ took place followed by other mystical phenomena that prompted her to open herself without hesitation to God's leading. In 1560 Teresa wrote her autobiography, *The Book of Her Life*. With a daring that would have been impossible without divine intervention, she chose to return to the original rule of Mount Carmel and to live the life of a reformed or

Discalced ("without shoes") cloistered Carmelite in the utter poverty of the Convent of Saint Joseph in Avila. Several daughters followed their "Mother," and the instructions she gave them can be found in her next book, *The Way of Perfection*. Teresa's courage and cheerful heart prevailed over all obstacles, and new convents arose, including one at Medina del Campo, where she met the friar who would understand her call and her spiritual life and who would join her in the reform, St. John of the Cross. In 1579, she wrote her masterpiece, *The Interior Castle*, but soon thereafter her strength waned and her health worsened. She received the last sacraments on October 3, 1582, and the next evening she met "his Majesty," Christ Jesus, whose servant she was. Never could she have imagined that on September 27, 1970, Pope Paul VI would proclaim her a Doctor of the Church, the first woman to be so honored.

THÉRÈSE OF LISIEUX, ST. (1873-1897). From 1877, when her mother died, to December 25, 1886, when she received, as she says in her autobiography, the grace of her complete conversion, Thérèse experienced a burning thirst for souls and the need to find peace of mind at the foot of the cross. At the age of fifteen, she acquired special permission to enter Carmel after the bold request she made of Pope Leo XIII. The name she chose to symbolize her new identity in Carmel beautifully expresses the charism of her life: Thérèse of the Child Jesus and the Holy Face. Though she had only nine more years to live before tuberculosis would claim her, Thérèse taught all of her sisters, and later the tens of thousands of people who embraced her as their strongest advocate in heaven, how to live a life of joyful abandonment to Divine Providence, how to turn even the smallest daily event into an occasion of grace, and how to change the darkest trial of suffering into a time of intense mystical transformation. A prolific letter writer and an exquisite poet, Thérèse agreed, under obedience, to write her life story, never knowing that it would become one of the most inspiring and best loved books of all ages. Though she never left the enclosure, she became the patroness of the missions of the whole world. She who saw herself as a grain of sand in the immensity of the ocean was, in the words of Pope Pius X, "the greatest saint of modern times." On World Mission Sunday, October 19, 1998, St. John Paul II named her a Doctor of the Church.

VAN KAAM, ADRIAN (1920-2007). Holland,
the home country of this modern-day spiritual master, research professor, Spiritan priest, and prolific author, fell under Nazi occupation in the 1940s. The horror of this experience made an indelible imprint on his spirit during the infamous Dutch Hunger Winter (1944-1945). Van Kaam, then a theology student, was trapped behind enemy lines in The Hague, the city of his birth. There, working with the underground, he helped Jews and Christians to hide from the Nazis. In the countryside around the village of Nieuwkoop — where, as a young theology student, he had consoled and counseled many suffering souls — he gathered whatever food he could for those in hiding. Their story became the experiential basis for his research, writing, and teaching in the art and discipline of formative and transformative spirituality. Some years after the war and following his ordination to the priesthood, van Kaam was appointed professor of philosophy at his seminary. At the same time, he accepted an invitation to teach in local mills and factories in a nationwide program devoted to the social and spiritual formation of young laborers. Shortly after completing these

assignments in the Netherlands, he was invited in 1954 to join the faculty of Duquesne University in Pittsburgh, where he pioneered his understanding of "psychology as a human science." In 1963, he founded the Institute of Man (later renamed the Institute of Formative Spirituality) at Duquesne University, but thirty years later the crowning phase of his life's work unfolded under the auspices of the Epiphany Association, a non-profit research and publication center co-founded by himself and his colleague, Doctor Susan Muto. Until shortly before his death, he remained actively involved in the Epiphany Academy of Formative Spirituality, where he completed his multi-volume series on the science, anthropology, and theology of formation. His life's work and legacy is an inspiration to students, researchers, and faithful followers of Christ throughout the world.

WILLIAM OF ST. THIERRY (1085-1148). A man of noble parentage, William was born in Liege, France. Thanks to his education and social standing, he could have pursued a worldly career, but he chose instead in 1121 to enter the nearby Benedictine monastery of Saint Thierry. There he served as the abbot for nearly fourteen years, providing exemplary spiritual leadership and integrating theological learning with the simplicity of living in a monastic community. Unable to perform manual labor because of his physically frail constitution, William devoted himself to writing. In 1135 he resigned his abbatial office and withdrew to the Cistercian monastery of Sygny, where he composed his two masterworks on the integration of belief and loving surrender to God: *The Enigma of Faith* and *The Mirror of Faith.* In 1144, after visiting the Carthusian monks of Mont-Dieu near Rheims, he composed *The Golden Epistle.* In it, he writes eloquently of the efficacy and effectiveness of the contemplative life and of the importance of receiving spiritual direction rooted in ascetical and mystical theology. Living the faith meant for William participating in the life of the Trinity here on earth, in anticipation of the Beatific Vision granted to us by God in the life to come.

BIBLIOGRAPHY

Aelred of Rievaulx. *Spiritual Friendship.* Translated by Mary
      Eugenia Laker. Washington, DC: Cistercian
      Publications, 1974.

Arndt, Johann. *True Christianity.* Translated by Peter Erb.
      New York: Paulist Press, 1979.

Bonaventure: The Soul's Journey into God. Translated by Ewert
      Cousins. New York: Paulist Press, 1978.

Bonhoeffer, Dietrich. *The Cost of Discipleship.* New York:
      Macmillan, 1963.

————. *Letters and Papers from Prison.* Eberhard Bethge,
      editor. New York: Macmillan, 1972.

Brother Lawrence of the Resurrection. *Writings and
      Conversations on the Practice of the Presence of God.*
      Conrad de Meester, editor. Washington, DC:
      Institute of Carmelite Studies, 1994.

Carretto, Carlo. *The Desert in the City.* Translated by Barbara
      Wall. New York: Collins, 1979.

Catherine of Siena. The Dialogue. Translated by Suzanne
      Noffke. New York: Paulist Press, 1980.

Ciszek, SJ. Walter J. with Daniel Flaherty. *He Leadeth Me*. San
       Francisco: Ignatius Press, 1973.

Confessions of St. Augustine. Translated by John K. Ryan.
       Garden City, NY: Image Books, 1960.

Day, Dorothy. *The Long Loneliness*. Garden City, NY: Image
       Books, 1959.

de Caussade, Jean-Pierre. *Abandonment to Divine Providence*.
       Translated by John Beevers. Garden City, NY:
       Image Books, 1975.

de Sales, Francis. *Introduction to the Devout Life*. Translated
       by John K. Ryan. Garden City, NY: Image Books,
       1972.

Elizabeth of the Trinity. *I Have Found God* in *The Complete
Works,* Volume I. Translated by Sister Aletheia Kane. Washington, DC: Institute of Carmelite Studies, 1984.

Francis and Clare: The Complete Works. Translated by Regis J.
       Armstrong and Ignatius C. Brady. New York:
       Paulist Press, 1982.

Gregory the Great. *Pastoral Care.* Translated by Henry
       Davis. New York: Newman Press, 1950.

Hadewijch, *The Complete Works* in *The Classics of Western
       Spirituality*. Translated by Mother Columba Hart.
       New York: Paulist Press, 1980.

Julian of Norwich. *Showings.* Translated by James Walsh.
       New York: Paulist Press, 1978.

Kelly, Thomas R. *A Testament of Devotion.* San Francisco: Harper Collins, 1992.

Law, William. *A Serious Call to a Devout and Holy Life: The Spirit of Love.* New York: Paulist Press, 1978.

LeFevre, Perry, editor. *The Prayers of Kierkegaard.* Chicago: The University of Chicago Press, 1956.

Letterman, Rebecca and Susan Muto. *Understanding Our Story: The Life's Work and Legacy of Adrian van Kaam.* Eugene, OR: Wipf & Stock, 2017.

Muto, Susan. *Blessings that Make Us Be: A Formative Approach to Living the Beatitudes.* Pittsburgh, PA: Epiphany Books, 2002.

_____. *Catholic Spirituality from A to Z: An Inspirational Dictionary.* Pittsburgh, Pennsylvania: Epiphany Books, 2005.

_____. *Keepsakes for the Journey: Four Weeks on Faith Deepening.* Hyde Park, NY: New City Press, 2010.

_____. *Meditation in Motion.* Pittsburgh, PA: Epiphany Books, 2001.

_____. *One in the Lord.* Hyde Park, NY: New City Press, 2013.

_____. *Pathways of Spiritual Living.* Pittsburgh, PA: Epiphany Books, 2004.

_____. *A Practical Guide to Spiritual Reading*. Petersham, MA: St. Bede's Publications, 1994.

_____. *Table of Plenty: Good Food for Body and Spirit*. Cincinnati, OH: Franciscan Media, 2014.

_____.*Twelve Little Ways to Transform Your Heart: Lessons in Holiness and Evangelization from St. Thérèse of Lisieux*. Notre Dame, IN: Ave Maria Press, 2016.

_____. *Virtues: Your Christian Legacy*. Steubenville, OH: Emmaus Road, 2014.

David O'Neal, editor. *Meister Eckhart from Whom God Hid Nothing: Sermons, Writings, and Sayings*. Boulder, CO: New Seeds Books, 1996.

Pseudo-Dionysius. *The Complete Works*. Translated by Colm Luibheid. New York: Paulist Press, 1987.

The Rule of St. Benedict. Timothy Fry, editor. Collegeville, MN: Liturgical Press, 1981.

The Sayings of Light and Love in *The Collected Works of St. John of the Cross*. Translated by Kieran Kavanagh and Otilio Rodriguez. Washington, DC: Institute of Carmelite Studies, 1991.

Seeds of Hope: A Henri Nouwen Reader. Robert Durback, editor. New York: Doubleday Image Books, 1997.

The Spiritual Canticle in *The Collected Works of St. John of the Cross*. Translated by Kieran Kavanaugh and Otilio

Rodriguez. Washington, DC: Institute of Carmelite Studies, 1991.

Steere, Douglas V. *Together in Solitude*. New York: Cross road, 1985.

Stein, Edith. *Finite and Eternal Being: An Attempt at an Ascent to the Meaning of Being* in *The Collected Works of Edith Stein*. Translated by Kurt F. Reinhardt. Washington, DC: Institute of Carmelite Studies, 2002.

Suso, Henry. *The Exemplar with Two German Sermons*. Translated by Frank Tobin. New York: Paulist Press, 1989.

Tauler, John. *Spiritual Conferences.* Translated by Eric Colledge and Sr. M. Jane. Rockford, IL: Tan Books and Publishers, 1978.

Ten Boom, Corrie. *The Hiding Place.* Grand Rapids, MI: Chosen Books, 1998.

Teresa of Avila. *The Way of Perfection* in *The Collected Works of St. Teresa of Avila.* Volume Two. Translated by Kieran Kavanaugh, and Otilio Rodriguez. Washington, DC: ICS Publications, 1980.

Thérèse of Lisieux, St. *Story of a Soul: The Autobiography of St. Thérèse of Lisieux*. Translated by John Clarke. Washington, DC: Institute of Carmelite Studies, 1975.

van Kaam, Adrian. *The Life Journey of a Joyful Man of God: The Autobiographical Memoirs of Adrian van Kaam*. Susan Muto, editor. Eugene, OR: Wipf & Stock, 2010.

_____. *The Roots of Christian Joy*. Denville, NJ: Dimension
        Books, 1985.

_____. *The Woman at the Well*. Pittsburgh, PA: Epiphany
        Books, 2004.

William of St. Thierry. *The Golden Epistle: A Letter to the
        Brethren at Mont Dieu*. Translated by Theodore
        Berkeley. Kalamazoo, MI: Cistercian Publication,
        1980.

***

***

NOTES

PART ONE

1.   Teresa of Avila, *The Way of Perfection* in *The Collected Works of St. Teresa of Avila*. Volume Two, translated by Kieran Kavanaugh and Otilio Rodriguez (Washington, DC: Institute of Carmelite Studies, 1980), Chapter 26:1, 133.

2.   Catherine of Siena, *The Dialogue*, translated by Suzanne Noffke (New York: Paulist Press, 1980), 29:70.

3.   John Tauler, *Spiritual Conferences*, translated by Eric Colledge and Sister M. Jane (Rockford, IL: Tan Books and Publishers, 1978), 206-207.

4.   Thérèse of Lisieux, *Story of a Soul: The Autobiography of St. Thérèse of Lisieux,* translated by John Clarke (Washington, DC: Institute of Carmelite Studies, 1975), X:207.

5.   Jean-Pierre de Caussade, *Abandonment to Divine Providence,* translated by John Beevers (Garden City, NY: Image Books, 1975), 70.

6.   Walter J. Ciszek, SJ with Daniel Flaherty. *He Leadeth Me* (San Francisco: Ignatius Press, 1973), 39.

7.   Carlo Carretto, *The Desert in the City*, translated by Barbara Wall (New York: Collins, 1979), 21.

8.   *Seeds of Hope: A Henri Nouwen Reader*, edited by Robert Durback (New York: Doubleday Image Books, 1997), 119.

9.   Dorothy Day, *The Long Loneliness* (Garden City, NY: Im-

age Books, 1959), 251.

10.   See Susan Muto, *Blessings that Make Us Be: A Formative Approach to Living the Beatitudes* (Pittsburgh, PA: Epiphany Books, 2002), Preface, xi-xvi.

11.   Bonaventure, *The Soul's Journey into God,* translated by Ewert Cousins (New York: Paulist Press, 1978), 59.

12.   Aelred of Rievaulx, *Spiritual Friendship,* translated by Mary Eugenia Laker (Washington, DC: Cistercian Publications, 1974), 129.

PART TWO

13.   *Meister Eckhart from Whom God Hid Nothing: Sermons, Writings, and Sayings,* ed. David O'Neal (Boulder, CO: New Seeds Books, 1996), 15.

14.   William Law, *A Serious Call to a Devout and Holy Life: The Spirit of Love* (New York: Paulist Press, 1978), 326.

15.   Brother Lawrence of the Resurrection, *Writings and Conversations on the Practice of the Presence of God,* edited by Conrad de Meester (Washington, DC: Institute of Carmelite Studies, 1994), Letter 3:57.

16.   Thomas R. Kelly, *A Testament of Devotion* (San Francisco: Harper Collins, 1992), 98.

17.   *The Sayings of Light and Love* in *The Collected Works of St. John of the Cross,* translated by Kieran Kavanagh and Otilio Rodriguez (Washington, DC: Institute of Carmelite Studies, 1991), Number 100:92.

18.   Elizabeth of the Trinity, *I Have Found God* in *The Complete Works,* Volume I, translated by Sister Aletheia Kane (Washington, DC: Institute of Carmelite Studies, 1984), 146.

19. *Confessions of St. Augustine*, translated by John K. Ryan (Garden City, NY: Image Books, 1960), Book 10, Chapter 27:254-255.

20.   Dietrich Bonhoeffer, *Letters and Papers from Prison*, edited by Eberhard Bethge (New York: Macmillan, 1972), 141-142.

21.   Adrian van Kaam. *The Roots of Christian Joy* (Denville, NJ: Dimension Books, 1985), 120.

22.   Julian of Norwich, *Showings*, translated by James Walsh (New York: Paulist Press, 1978), 254.

PART THREE

23.   *The Rule of St. Benedict*, edited by Timothy Fry (Collegeville, MN: The Liturgical Press, 1981), Chapter 5:187.

24.   Bonaventure, *The Soul's Journey into God*, translated by Ewert Cousins (New York: Paulist Press, 1978), 63.

25.   *The Prayers of Kierkegaard*, ed. Perry D. LeFevre (Chicago: The University of Chicago Press, 1956), 105.

26.   William of St. Thierry, *The Golden Epistle: A Letter to the Brethren at Mont Dieu*, translated by Theodore Berkeley (Kalamazoo, MI: Cistercian Publications, 1980), 93.

27.   Hadewijch, *The Complete Works*, translated by Mother Columba Hart (New York: Paulist press, 1980), 80.

28.   Hadewijch, 80.

29.   Gregory the Great, *Pastoral Care*, translated by Henry Davis (New York: Newman Press, 1950), 237.

30.   *The Spiritual Canticle* in *The Collected Works of St. John of the Cross*, translated by Kieran Kavanaugh and Otilio Rodriguez (Washington, DC: Institute of Carmelite Studies, 1991), Stanza 1:3,

479.

31.   Dietrich Bonhoeffer, *The Cost of Discipleship* (New York: Macmillan, 1963), 103.

32.   Pseudo-Dionysius, *The Complete Works*, translated by Colm Luibheid (New York: Paulist Press, 1987), 254.

33.   Edith Stein, *Finite and Eternal Being: An Attempt at an Ascent to the Meaning of Being* in *The Collected Works of Edith Stein*, translated by Kurt F. Reinhardt (Washington, DC: Institute of Carmelite Studies, 2002), 113.

34.   *Francis and Clare, The Complete Works*, translated by Regis J. Armstrong and Ignatius E. Brady (New York: Paulist Press, 1982), 204.

PART FOUR

35.   *Henry Suso, The Exemplar with* Two German Sermons, translated by Frank Tobin (New York: Paulist Press, 1989), 353-354.

36.   Jean-Pierre de Caussade, *Abandonment to* Divine Providence, translated by John Beevers (Garden City, NY: Image Books, 1975), 40-41.

37.   Walter J. Ciszek, SJ, with *Daniel Flaherty. He Leadeth Me* (San Francisco: Ignatius Press, 1973), 45.

38.   Douglas V. Steere, *Together in Solitude* (New York: Crossroad, 1985), 177.

39.   Johann Arndt, *True Christianity*, translated by Peter Erb (New York: Paulist Press, 1979), 180.

40.   Corrie Ten Boom, *The Hiding Place* (Grand Rapids, MI: Chosen Books, 1998), 206.

41.   Thérèse of Lisieux, *Story of a Soul: The Autobiography of*

St. Thérèse of Lisieux, translated by John Clarke (Washington, DC: Institute of Carmelite Studies, 1975), IX:195.

42.   Francis de Sales, *Introduction to the Devout Life*, translated by John K. Ryan (Garden City, NY: Image Books, 1972), 174-175.

<u>EPILOGUE</u>

43.   *See Rebecca Letterman and Susan Muto, Understanding Our Story: The* Life's Work and Legacy of Adrian van Kaam *(Eugene, OR: Wipf & Stock, 2017). See also The Life's Journey of a Joyful Man of God: The* Autobiographical Memoirs of Adrian van Kaam, ed. Susan Muto (Eugene: OR: Wipf & Stock, 2010).

ABOUT THE AUTHOR

S usan Muto, Ph.D., is execu-
tive director of the Epiphany
Association, based in Pittsburgh,
Pennsylvania, and dean of the
Epiphany Academy of Formative
Spirituality. She holds a doctorate
in English literature from the University of Pittsburgh, where she
specialized in the work of post–
Reformation spiritual writers. Be-
ginning in 1966, she served in various administrative and
teaching positions at the Institute of Formative Spirituality
(IFS) at Duquesne University.

Dr. Muto has been teaching the literature of ancient,
medieval, and modern spirituality for over forty years. She
has written many books, including companion texts to the
masterpieces of St. John of the Cross. She has also recorded popular audio series. All of these resources are available
from the Epiphany Association (877-324-6873).

Her articles have appeared in *Spiritual Life Magazine*,
Mount Carmel, *The Pittsburgh Catholic*, and *Human Development*. She has written more than forty books, many of them
co-authored with Father Adrian van Kaam. She lectures in-
ternationally on the Judeo–Christian formation tradition.

In 2014 she received the Aggiornamento Award presented by the Catholic Library Association in recognition of
an outstanding contribution made by an individual or an
organization to the ministry of renewal modeled by Pope
St. John XXIII.

OTHER BOOKS BY SUSAN MUTO

Approaching the Sacred: An Introduction to Spiritual Reading

Blessings That Make Us Be: A Formative Approach to Living the Beatitudes

Caring for the Caregiver

Catholic Spirituality A to Z: An Inspirational Dictionary

Celebrating the Single Life: A Spirituality for Single Persons in Today's World

Dear Master: Letters on Spiritual Direction Inspired by St. John of the Cross

Deep Into the Thicket: Soul Searching Meditations Inspired by The Spiritual Canticle of St. John of the Cross

Gratefulness: The Habit of a Grace-Filled Life

John of the Cross for Today: The Ascent

John of the Cross for Today: The Dark Night

Keepsakes for the Journey: Four Weeks on Faith Deepening

The Journey Homeward: On the Road of Spiritual Reading

Late Have I Loved Thee: The Recovery of Intimacy

Meditation in Motion

One in the Lord: Living the Call to Christian Community

Pathways of Spiritual Living

A Practical Guide to Spiritual Reading

Readings from A to Z: The Poetry of Epiphany

Praying the Lord's Prayer with Mary

Renewed at Each Awakening

Steps Along the Way: The Path of Spiritual Reading

Table of Plenty: Good Food for Body and Spirit

Then God Said: Contemplating The First Revelation in Creation

Twelve Little Ways to Transform Your Heart: Lessons in Holiness and Evangelization from St. Thérèse of Lisieux

Virtues: Your Christian Legacy

Where Lovers Meet: Inside the Interior Castle

Womanspirit: Reclaiming the Deep Feminine in our Human Spirituality

Words of Wisdom for Our World: The Precautions and Counsels of St. John of the Cross